Table Of Contents

Personal Development 101

Personal growth is a trendy issue and has been for a while, but things are changing in this area! who makes up today's largest population? Millennials. Who today is the largest demographic engaged in personal growth? Women.

You will find a lot of middle-aged folks, mostly guys, giving advise on videos or in books if you go back a decade or two. That's perfectly OK; the key is that the personal development sector as a whole feels far more inclusive now than it did in the past. For everyone, young or old, who wants to accept growth, it is a good thing.

Personal growth may have formerly been dismissed as new-age rubbish, but today it is supported by science and study. As a result, its popularity has quickly increased. Another significant component that has increased everyone's access to personal growth is technology.

By clicking a button, you can access a variety of material, including blogs, articles, videos, and more. Let's take a moment to define personal growth and describe what it looks like if you're not sure if it's good for you. It is applicable to every aspect of your life and even your workplace culture. It is for everyone.

You can evaluate your traits and skills and work to improve them in order to define and meet goals through personal development. Your potential is limitless, and personal growth will help you realize it. This trip lasts a lifetime.

The procedure will assist you in focusing on the abilities you require to accomplish your life goals as well as the steps necessary to acquire those particular abilities. Any sort of personal development typically has the side effect of increasing your self-esteem and confidence. Whether you choose to aspire for those two things or not, this is true.

As you embark on a journey of personal development, you will enhance your skills, improve your chances at employability, boost your confidence, and most importantly, it will help you find fulfillment. If you want to feel empowered then you need to plan positive, effective, and relevant decisions and choices.

While your school career may end with some type of degree, the personal development process does not end until you leave this mortal coil. At least, it shouldn't! We are constantly growing and evolving as we age and you can either let it go as is or you can steer the direction in which you grow and evolve by consciously focusing on your personal development journey. With that in mind, let me touch on why personal development is so important.

Self-Actualization

There are many concepts related to human development, but self-actualization may be the most prevalent—or at the very least, the most well-known.

American psychologist Abraham Maslow developed the hierarchy of needs that most people are familiar with. This theory is predicated on the premise that we all have fundamental desires, and that there is a hierarchy in which we achieve them, with self-actualization at the top.

The extent to which you are able to develop will all depend on needs being met and all of those needs merge together into a hierarchy (of needs). When you satisfy the level of needs at the bottom, you can address the next level, and so on.

At the very bottom level of the hierarchy, you will find your physiological needs. It's the basics that you need for survival – air, shelter, clothing, sleep, food, and drinks.

The second level is both economic and physical, you need both security and safety.

At the third level, you seek friendships and relationships. It's about inclusion and belonging.

The fourth level is meeting your needs for self-worth and self-esteem. This could be combined to create self-empowerment. It's about feeling accomplished.

Self-actualization is lastly at the very top of the ladder. Finding your mission is motivated by your desire for progress and clarity as well as your natural curiosity. The desire to become what we are capable of being is known as self-actualization. Realizing your greatest potential is it.

That was the initial hierarchy, it was later expanded (by Maslow himself) to include *eight* levels. Below, you will find the additional three, but know that in the expanded model self-actualization becomes the second top to the ultimate need which is transcendence.

First, the added need is aesthetic, we search for and appreciate beauty and balance.

The second is cognitive needs. It's the search for meaning to find knowledge and understanding.

Finally, transcendence needs. People are motivated by their values and those values transcend your personal self. This includes serving others, pursuing science, faith and spirituality, and even sexual experiences.

In the expanded model, we see the hierarchy split into two sections. The bottom four levels are made up of what are classed as deficiency needs, with the upper four levels falling under the umbrella of growth (https://www.simplypsychology.org/maslow.html#needs7).

Managing Personal Development

Before we get into all of the different personal development ideas and goals, I want to help you how to manage the process.

Develop Your Personal Vision

While some people do work on themselves for fun, it's much easier to maintain long-term motivation for personal development if you have a purpose. So, take a moment to develop your vision. It should be a clear picture or idea of where you want to be and perhaps most importantly, *why* you want that.

Areas Of Life And Self In Consideration Of Self-Improvement

- Mental/Psychological
- Emotional
- Social/Relationships
- Professional/Work
- Spiritual
- Recreational
- Physical
- Lifestyle
- Spiritual Development

Plan It

You may begin making plans for how you will get there once you have a clear idea of where you want to be. Although it is not necessary, including this in your personal growth plan will help it feel more real.

Use The Model of S.M.A.R.T. Goals In Your Planning

- Specific
- Measurable
- Attainable
- Relevant
- Time-Bound

Begin The Process Of Self-Improvement

You can learn and develop in all different ways, as you start the development process you can explore and experiment with how you prefer to learn. The process is highly personal and should reflect what is best for you.

Examples Of Methods To Engage In Self-Improvement

- Therapy
- Support Groups
- Life Coaches
- Read About What You Want To Improve

- Find A Mentor
- Create A Practice Routine
- Stay Consistent In Your Endeavors And Plan
- Be Honest With Yourself
- Journal
- Find Like Minded People With Same Goals

Record And Track Your Progress

It's a good idea to keep track of your progress. You can think back on your main development points afterwards by writing notes on them. The opportunity to see the results of your efforts that come from tracking your personal improvement is a great tool for keeping you motivated to keep going. Considering that self-improvement is a continuous process, finding constructive ways to motivate yourself is essential.

Methods to Track Your Progress

- Journal your journey. Make notes on your key developmental points so you can reflect on them often.
- Notice positive changes in your life as a result of your work
- Check in with yourself regularly as to the issue you are working on

- Stay accountable share your progress with a friend or therapist

Review And Revise

Learning is a process and a cycle. Continued review and revision keeps your growing. Reassessing as to what is working and what is not helps you replan steps to reach your goals.

- Review and revise your plans, activities, and ideas often to ensure that you're on the right track.
- Once you have conquered a goal, check it off your list.
- Reevaluate steps to each goal and make changes as needed.

Rules Of Personal Development

1. It's never too late to start actively working on your personal growth.

2. Personal development can be useful even if you don't need it.

3. Personal development doesn't require you to be unhappy or unfulfilled in order to be beneficial.

4. There is no one right technique to approach personal development.

5. Your path to personal development is unique to you and won't resemble anybody else's. Therefore, what is effective for one person may not be effective for another.

6. Resources for personal development are not all created equal.

7. Just because you experience failure does not mean you should stop. You just have to find something else that works for you.

8. Personal development doesn't end, once you reach one goal, you set another. It's a process that will last your lifetime.

9. Personal development can be uncomfortable and it takes time, effort, and maybe even some blood, sweat, and tears.

10. It's never too late to start making progress on your personal development.

11. You don't have to be in need of it to gain from personal growth.

12. Personal development might be helpful even if you're not unhappy or unfulfilled.

13. Personal development cannot be done in a single, effective approach.

14. There will be nothing similar about your personal development journey to anyone else's. This implies that while something may work for a friend, it might not for you.

15. Various tools are available for personal development.

Personal Development Ideas And Goals

Personal development is possible for every area of your life. With that in mind, you will find 100 personal development ideas and goals below and which area of your life they can be filed under. Under each idea or goal, you will also find some action steps to take to make it happen!

Personal Self-Improvement

There are lots of goals and ideas you can use to drive your personal development. By building self-esteem, you contribute to your personal development. By organizing your home, you contribute to your personal development. That being said, there are still more direct goals and ideas that drive your personal development, and this section is dedicated to *those* specific ideas and goals.

Gratitude

What better way to grow as a person than by learning how to be grateful for everything you have. You might not have the car that you want, but if you have a car then you are getting from point a to point b.

You wish your house were bigger, but you have a roof over your head. In an ideal world, you'd be eating surf and turf every night, but that's not healthy and you go to bed with a full belly. There are many benefits to gratitude, it improves your physical health, increases empathy, boosts self-esteem, helps build better relationships, and it will even help you sleep better!

- I want you to think about the worst thing that's ever happened to you and try to find one single positive that came from that situation. This doesn't remove the sadness, anger, or disappointment from an event or situation, it just forces you to look at things a little differently.

  For example, if you experience the loss of a loved one, it's difficult to overlook your grief and pain to find a silver lining and why would you want to?

  But there is a really obvious thing that you can be grateful for and that is that you got to know that person at all. That doesn't mean you immediately let go of your grief or just get over it. It's about focusing on the most positive aspect you can find. You can't bring them back, but you can celebrate the life they lived and the moments you shared.

I chose the most extreme example because I know how most people react when someone encourages them to find the silver lining. It elicits an eye roll and a heavy sigh. How do you find a silver lining to a terminal diagnosis? You can be grateful for the foresight that will allow you to use the rest of your time wisely. Again, it doesn't remove the pain or help you heal, but it can help you live life to its fullest.

☐ Every morning before you get out of bed, come up with one reason you are grateful for the day ahead.

☐ Every evening before you go to sleep, think of one thing you are grateful for.

Give Up On Perfection

Being perfect is a lie. The stunning models you see on social media are stunning, but their images have been airbrushed and face-retouched. Their skin isn't as flawless, their teeth aren't as white, and their tan isn't as even or dark as it seems. It's holding you back from trying to compete with that or aspire to that. If you constantly contrast yourself with others in an effort to achieve perfection, you cannot be happy.

I want to emphasize the difference between "healthy" and "unhealthy" perfectionism. We'll concentrate on personal pleasure in this example. Celebrating all of your victories and giving yourself credit when you deserve it would be healthy perfection. Unhealthy perfection is the state of being perpetually unsatisfied with your accomplishments and believing that they are insufficient. Health perfectionism would be the capacity to perceive the big picture and put out the necessary effort to complete tasks on a macro as opposed to micro level. An unhealthy perfectionism would prevent you from seeing the big picture because you would be too preoccupied with the workings.

Another good example of healthy perfectionism versus unhealthy perfectionism is a failure. It's healthy to reflect on your failures and learn a lesson to apply moving forward. It's unhealthy to constantly beat yourself up over past mistakes.

Now, understand that what I've classed as healthy perfectionism isn't perfectionism at all, it's personal growth. That's your goal.

☐ What is the biggest perfectionism issue that you have? What is one thing you can do right now to pop a hole in it? If you spend half an hour drafting a simple email, then you can start there. Perhaps you feel angry when someone close to you experiences success? That's another good place to start because it speaks to your perfectionism and to something a little deeper. Go out of your way to be imperfect today.

☐ How do you proceed after day one? In much the same way, the only way to break the habit of perfectionism is to be proactive.

Find A Life Coach

Since we've already talked about how beneficial a mentor can be to your work, the presence of a life coach on this list shouldn't come as a surprise to you. The purpose of a life coach is to assist you in overcoming the constraints you have imposed on yourself. A life coach should encourage you to develop and assist you in creating the life you've always wanted. In the end, they will assist you in creating a plan to make things happen by assisting you in identifying hurdles, strengthening relationships, enhancing job prospects, and clarifying goals.

A life coach may assist you in becoming prepared to handle particular situations, which is one of the advantages of having one. A life coach can assist you in being more present if you want to. Do you want to work harder and be more successful? A life coach can also assist you with that.

Most persons who have worked with a life coach thought it was worthwhile and would be interested in hiring their services again if necessary.

☐ What do you do now? First things first, speak to the people in your life who may be able to recommend a life coach. If you don't know anyone, there are plenty of online forums and reviews to read that will give you a better idea of who will match your needs and requirements.

☐ Before you meet with your life coach, write out a brief outline of your ideas for your life. What do you want from this experience? What do you want from life? What do your goals look like, what areas of your life would you like to work on? Go into your meeting with an open mind and be prepared for the challenge ahead.

Build Self-Awareness

What is the relationship between self-awareness and personal development? Knowing your own worth and principles is important, as is comprehending your needs, personality, emotions, habits, shortcomings, and talents. It involves learning how to control your stress, inspire yourself, and develop your decision-making abilities. It is one of the most effective personal growth tools you can use, but you must first cultivate it. When you focus on your thoughts, you might begin to see how your beliefs influence your actions.

[] The advantages of self-awareness are numerous. It will increase your capacity for empathy, offer you more self-control, aid in decision-making, make it simpler to form good habits and break bad ones, and enhance your listening abilities. So let's start immediately to develop self-awareness.

[] Analyze your own actions with objectivity. Although it can be challenging, you can see yourself for who you really are with the correct effort. Write down your opinions about who you are, what you need to improve on, and what you excel at.

What are you particularly proud of? What made you happy in your childhood? Has that changed? Why? How? It's all about gaining a new or different perspective.

☐ Start by keeping a journal. By keeping a journal, you will have a tool to reflect on your thoughts, you can then reflect on those entries discover insights you might not otherwise notice. Always look for patterns, that's where the good stuff is.

☐ Write out your plans, priorities, and goals.

☐ Make time for daily self-reflection.

☐ Practice mindfulness habits.

☐ Ask close friends and family members to describe you and see how that aligns with your own perception of yourself.

☐ If you're feeling brave after all of that, then you can ask your boss and coworkers for anonymous feedback. You're not always the same person at work as you are at home or around your friends and family. It's always worth getting additional insight.

☐ Finally, I would suggest that you make a list of the things that annoy you about others. Often, we react with distaste to the qualities in others that we share. It annoys you so much in them because you know that it's true of you.

Forgive & Forget

Because they don't think others deserve their forgiveness, many people find the thought that they need to forgive frustrating. If you have the same view, I can see where you're coming from, but I'm here to tell you that forgiveness is about you, not forgiving others. You choose to let go of the hurt and animosity you have been carrying onto when you choose to forgive.

Are there in fact advantages to forgiving someone? Yes. Relationships can become healthier as a result of forgiveness, as can your mental health, blood pressure, stress levels, and anxiety levels. Ultimately, all of those things suffer if you harbor anger, bitterness, sadness, or grief. You let everything go by being forgiving.

☐ Honesty is the first step. You need to be honest about the level of hurt, anger, and sadness you have been holding onto in order to assess the damage it has had on you and your life. For example, you may have had a teacher who made you feel wholly inadequate and as a result, you struggle with your self-esteem. As a result, you seek validation and love in unhealthy places and damaging ways.

☐ You have to make a conscious decision to forgive the person who you believe wronged you. Part of that is letting go of ideas of vengeance or revenge. For example, five years ago your co-worker stole your idea, and ever since then you have refused to credit them for the work they have contributed. By choosing to forgive them you also give up the tactic of pursuing petty vengeance.

☐ Try to put yourself in their shoes and exercise empathy. You might never be able to understand why they caused you the pain they did, but you're coming from a place of assuming the harm was intentional. While impact might

be greater than intent, you can't let their
actions trap you in a cycle of anger.

- Try to find some meaning in the situation you
  have been through.

- You don't need to reach out to someone to
  offer forgiveness. It's different if someone who
  wronged you reaches out to apologize and ask
  for forgiveness.

Fill Your Glass

Do you tend to see things through a glass that's half
full or half empty? It's never too late to start seeing
the glass as half full if you're still working on it. You
can learn to be optimistic. You can learn yourself to
think more positively, which will make you happy
overall. Of course, being optimistic can also increase
your money and improve your health, in addition to
making you happier. How does that function? So,
when you hope for positive results, you act in a way
that helps those results happen. So let's
concentrate on fostering your positivism.

- You can start your journey by setting your
  intention. Before you even step foot out of bed,
  take a moment to set your intention for the day

ahead. There are all different ways you can do this, but to start, choose a single word that resonates with the energy, spirit, or attitude you want to carry throughout your day. This will act as your compass and hopefully, help you focus your energy and time more effectively.

As an example, your job search is frustrating and it's difficult to maintain your optimism. Well, your intention for the day would be proactive and your goal can be to submit at least five resumes or follow up on five different opportunities or leads.

☐ One great way to change your circumstances is to take courage. It's about closing the gap between your current position and where you'd like to be and that means action. It's time to jump out of your comfort zone and do something that scares you.

☐ Is there a problem that you are dealing with right now? How can you reframe it so you see it as an opportunity instead?

☐ Both optimism and pessimism are contagious so you should do your best to limit your contact with the pessimists that only drain your energy.

- Start carrying yourself like the optimist you want to become. Stand up straight, be a confident, optimistic, outgoing person.

- Stop taking yourself so seriously.

- Exercise makes you feel better, both physically and psychologically, so get exercising!

Adopt An Abundant Mindset

A person with an abundance of thought loves competition, has faith in other people, and is upbeat about the future. They understand that there are always winners and losers in life. Because there is plenty for everyone, there can be more than one winner. For instance, there is enough oxygen for everyone to breathe, therefore there is no need for us to compete for it.

You feel in charge of your life and in the driver's seat if you have an abundant mindset. Your level of engagement, sense of empowerment, and general outlook on life will all increase. Those are some very wonderful advantages, but before you can take use of them, you must focus on developing an abundant mindset.

- You need to think big! Abundant mindsets are all about big picture thinking. So, set a big goal to chase and start believing that you're capable of achieving it.

- We already discussed the importance of finding the good in any situation. This is an important part of cultivating an abundance mindset.

- Practicing gratitude is another important part of developing an abundance mindset.

- When an opportunity presents itself, look at it through optimistic eyes. You need to recognize that there are plenty of opportunities to be had, and there is enough for everyone. You can start by changing your language. *I can do it, I will do it, I have it, I'll get it, I've got this*, etc.

  These encouraging words prepare your subconscious and support the development of self-belief. Even if it's something you also want, you should be delighted for someone close to you when they accomplish something. The mere fact that they have it doesn't exclude you from doing so. Others' success does not equate to failure for you.

- You have to believe there are opportunities for everyone, but you still have to be proactive. You can't sit back and wait for it to come to you.

- Keep an open mind because you never know where an opportunity will come from.

Positive Affirmations

The topic of whether or not using positive affirmations is beneficial has received a lot of attention. You must truly believe positive affirmations in order for them to work. Repeating ideas or phrases that resonate with you will increase their likelihood of being beneficial.

For instance, if you tell yourself often that you are calm and capable and that you think this about yourself, you will discover that this reminder is helpful when there is confusion or conflict.

But if you keep saying, "I make money effortlessly," even though you've previously struggled with it, it won't work because you won't actually believe it.

You can use these encouraging words to combat negative thinking, stop self-destructive behavior, and bring about positive transformation. One of the most important advantages of using positive affirmations regularly is that they can assist you in reprogramming your mindset and banishing unfavorable thoughts. Your brain will immediately begin to repair those negative thoughts, so you won't even have to consider doing so.

- To get started, you will need to think of some truths you know about yourself that your mind often attempts to derail. You know you're good at your job, for example, but your brain is constantly whispering lies about you being awful at your job. What is your most common negative thought or self-sabotaging suggestion that drags you down?

- To begin, take a few deep breaths. As you inhale deeply count to six and then exhale to the count of seven.

- Look yourself in the eye as you stand in front of the mirror.

- Slowly, clearly, say your affirmation aloud. Repeat it five times and focus on the meaning and intention of each word in your affirmation.

- To finish, take a few deep breaths. As you inhale deeply, count to six and allow the positive vibes of your affirmation to absorb, and exhale to the count of seven.

- While you can repeat your affirmations at any time, especially when you can feel stress or anxiety bubbling up, it's always a good idea to set aside time each day to run through your affirmations. They will be more powerful when you need them if you "practice" them when you don't.

Motivate Yourself

Motivation is not limitless and cannot be acquired once and retained indefinitely. Zig Ziglar compared it like taking a shower; it's something you have to do every day. You might be unsure of the point, which is why I want to emphasize the advantages. Obviously, achieving your goals is the main advantage of self-motivation. Beyond that, self-motivation offers you direction, aids in overcoming indecision and unfavorable influences, expands your thinking, and provides you the strength to face any difficulty or difficult circumstance. The current question is how to develop self-motivation.

- Start by focusing your energy. If you want to motivate yourself then you need to avoid distractions to prevent a feeling of overwhelm. Simplifying things will help you make space. So, rather than pursuing multiple goals at once just choose one to work on at a time.

- Once you have your goals, choose one to work on and break it down into smaller steps. It's easier to maintain your motivation if you are constantly achieving and have something to celebrate until you reach your next milestone.

- You must be careful to control your expectations. You will encounter difficulties and roadblocks, and progress might not be as swift as you would like. You have to keep in mind that it's just a glitch and try not to let annoyance turn into despair.

- The people around you should be supportive because sometimes you need help getting back up. Know which people in your circle are the supportive types to lean on.

- Never be ashamed to ask for assistance if you require it. Gratitude might assist you in keeping your motivation high.

- Don't forget to celebrate your successes. When all of your dedication and hard work pays off, you deserve to grab the glory. Spend a brief minute reveling in your status as a rock star.

Adopt Supportive Habits

Although motivation is crucial, it will be useless if you can't adopt helpful practices. The choice between following your aspirations and staying in your comfort zone and watching life pass you by can be made by developing healthy, empowering habits.

Stress reduction and anchoring are two advantages of these helpful practices. In the end, sustaining habits provide routine, which grounds you. Regardless of the circumstances in your life, you always eat dinner at 5:30 and go to bed at 10.

Although motivation is crucial, it will be useless if you can't adopt helpful practices. The choice between following your aspirations and staying in your comfort zone and watching life pass you by can be made by developing healthy, empowering habits.

Stress reduction and anchoring are two advantages of these helpful practices. In the end, sustaining habits provide routine, which grounds you. Regardless of the circumstances in your life, you always eat dinner at 5:30 and go to bed at 10.

That type of routine and habit provides comfort and can be helpful for managing the uncertainty that life often brings. Supportive habits include a sleep routine, a daily routine, a healthy diet, and exercise. Let's talk about how you can adopt those.

- What are your top priorities in life? Make a list of the biggest three.

- What are your biggest stressors in life? Make a list of the biggest three.

- Now is your chance to come up with some daily routines that will support your priorities and help you eliminate or at the very least manage stressors. The simplest method to determine what qualifies as a supporting habit is to answer where you frequently undermine yourself and what intentions or ideas you secretly harbor.

- A helpful habit is anything that aids in addressing self-sabotage or promotes your ideas. You can only know exactly what to do if your behaviors are both measurable and explicit.

☐ I'd like to mention a handful to spark your imagination before you decide on your supportive routines. A helpful practice is setting aside 15 minutes each day to spend alone or with your partner in peaceful conversation. A helpful practice is to keep one diary where you record the entirety of your schedule.
Taking breaks, hydrating properly, keeping a consistent routine, and not taking your lunch at your desk are all great examples of supportive habits.

☐ Once you've selected a few helpful behaviors to practice, you should think of a perk for each one. Always keep in mind why you are developing these habits and how they will benefit you.

☐ You can now do something.

Monitor Your Media Consumption

There is nothing wrong with taking pleasure in television and online activities. Both can be useful tools, and having access to both fun and knowledge is convenient. There are many advantages to controlling your media intake. You'll become more self-aware, but you'll also feel less lonely, have more time to be more productive, be able to focus better, have a clearer sense of perspective, and have more self-esteem.

Particularly passive activities like watching TV are unlikely to be consistent with your ideals. Television ought to be a means of unwinding rather than a source of anxiety or procrastination. Take proactive measures to limit it if this is something you deal with.

☐ Before you can limit your media consumption you will need to figure out just how much of your time is spent watching television. So, when does the television go on and when do you turn it off?

☐ I'm sure you have favorite shows you're invested in. Put them in your schedule and make them part of your media consumption routine. Anything else? Should go.

☐ The same applies to how you utilize social media. There's no need to open your apps again or flip between them in search of fresh updates to your timeline. Give yourself two set periods every day to check social media, then abstain from it the rest of the time. This is challenging because many people have a propensity of opening them when bored. You'll need to find things to do, but you might also require a tool to prevent you from accessing social media outside of your permitted window of time.

Meditation

One of the most effective methods for achieving happiness and reducing stress is meditation. It is recognized for its ability to reduce the signs of anxiety and sadness and for its positive effects on both your physical and mental wellbeing. It's easy to get information overload because everyday information intake is so great and life can be overwhelming. Perspective, stress management, self-awareness, the capacity to stay in the present, the ability to combat bad emotions, the capacity to be more creative and innovative, and increased tolerance are just a few of the emotional advantages of meditation.

In terms of the body, asthma, chronic pain, anxiety, depression, gastrointestinal problems, headaches, high blood pressure, and sleep disturbances are just a few conditions that are frequently treated with meditation.

There are many distinct styles of meditation; the term "meditation" is used to refer to any activity that induces relaxation. There are numerous types of meditation, including mantra, guided, and mindfulness. You can achieve this state of relaxation through a variety of meditation techniques, each of which has a unique set of benefits.

There are common features that run throughout most types of meditation, these include a quiet setting, focused attention, an open mind, and relaxed breathing.

☐ Breathe deeply. Most meditations begin with deep breathing and it's something that you can do anywhere which means it's a great way to meditate wherever you are.

☐ Body scanning is another excellent technique. Simply focus your attention on a section of your body at a time and note the sensations. Combined with breathing exercises you can breathe out your stress.

- A mantra can be a meditative practice as when you repeat it you can do so in time with your breathing. Om is a mantra often used during yoga.

- You can meditate while you walk, especially if you do so in a tranquil spot. Rather than thinking about your destination, focus instead on your feet and legs carrying you through nature. You can add an action word that you repeat with every lift and step of your foot.

Break Out Of Your Comfort Zone

If you lack the bravery to leave your comfort zone, you will never be able to advance and change. You need to try new things if you want to develop as a person. When we are under duress, we develop. When we are under duress, we develop. Consider your life as a rock polisher and yourself as a rock. When pebbles are thrown into a polisher, they tumble around and clatter together with grit before emerging polished and gorgeous.

For them to emerge as the finished product, they needed to be stirred up. You need challenges in your life because they help you grow stronger and more resilient.

The advantages of leaving your comfort zone? It increases your productivity, resilience, adaptability, and self-awareness. It also helps you become a better person.

☐ If you want to break out of your comfort zone, then you start by changing your daily routine. Routine is an important part of building supportive habits, but you can still break out of certain parts of your routine to avoid the comfort zone.

For example, you can take a walk for pleasure, you can pick up a book rather than watching the news, you can park a mile from work and walk the rest of the way, or order something from the menu you would normally never try!

☐ Are you the type of person that prefers to complete chores on their own? Because you don't trust people to do things right, you frequently take on too much. Try giving some of the chores to others. There is no better way to leave your comfort zone than to let go. It lessens your workload, it pushes you outside of your comfort zone, and it allows others a chance to demonstrate their abilities. Whether at business or at home, delegation also positions you in a mentoring capacity.

☐ Make it a point to educate yourself today. Read a book you wouldn't typically pick up, take a class at the neighborhood community college, go horseback riding, learn a new language, or master a musical instrument. Growth requires discomfort as a necessary component.

Know Yourself

Are you clear on your life goals? If you give a negative response or exhibit any ambivalence, there's a significant possibility you'll end up in unfavorable area. Not to mention the fact that it is challenging to concentrate on your own development when you are unsure of the route you want to take it. This can be avoided.

Why is it important that you are aware of yourself? There is more to adore the more you learn. Being an independent thinker is easier the more you understand yourself. Are you clear on your life goals? If you give a negative response or exhibit any ambivalence, there's a significant possibility you'll end up in an unfavorable area. Not to mention the fact that it is challenging to concentrate on your own development when you are unsure of the route you want to take it. This can be avoided.

Why is it necessary to be conscious of who you are? The more you know, the more there is to love. The more self-aware you become, the easier it will be to think independently.

You understand yourself well enough to know what you think, believe, or value, so you don't need to hear what others say. Knowing yourself also aids in decision-making. When you are certain of who you are and what you want, there is no need to second-guess yourself.

☐ You should first take a seat and consider the previous 12 months. Do you enjoy the course you're going in? Do you like the direction you are going in? What can you improve upon? What more should you do? What ought to you lessen? What routines and interests help you achieve your goals? Do you give yourself enough downtime to recharge after a stressful day?

☐ Every period of reflection is a chance to know yourself on a deeper level. The more you question and challenge yourself, the more you hone in on exactly who you are and what you want. It doesn't have to be a complicated process, you simply have to stick with it.

 From this point forward, you can perform the reflection process once a year at the very least. The best time to do it is at the end of the year because it will be simpler to manage. You don't have to wait a whole year, though.

If you'd like, you can engage in reflection exercises quarterly, twice a year, or even weekly. It's about doing what suits you the best.

Write A Mission Statement

You can either create a goal statement for your entire life or for a certain aspect of it. You can focus on your priorities by creating a mission statement, which is a wonderful way to develop decision-making abilities.

What justifies creating a mission statement? since there are countless advantages! Your why can be clearly expressed in your mission statement. Now who are you? Whom do you want to be? You may maintain focus on your desires and objectives by using your mission statement. It's a fantastic tool for keeping you on course.

You can either write out your overall life goals or specific goals for each area. Making a mission statement allows you to focus on your priorities, which is a great method to improve your ability to make decisions.

Why should a mission statement be written? since there are so many benefits! Your mission statement can succinctly explain your why. Who are you now? Who do you aspire to become? By employing your mission statement, you may keep your attention on your goals and desires. It's an excellent tool for helping you stay on track. Your mission statement can serve as a helpful reminder to consider the larger picture when you are facing a challenging situation. Shut out the noise, forget the complications and difficulty of life, you're working towards something bigger.

As a result of your decisions needing to be in line with your mission statement, it will also assist you in streamlining the decision-making process. You'll be able to live out your vision and be happy as a result. Here are the steps for you;

- Write down the things that are most significant to you first. What do you hold dear? You value whom? What are your top priorities? What do you feel strongly about? How are these people and things related to your life?

  - Think on your most important objectives, both professional and personal. What would the ideal version of your life look like, if you could only picture it?

  - What traits would you desire to be perceived as having by others?

  - What do you want out of your career?

  - What goals do you have for yourself (personally, professionally, etc.)?

- Talk to the people around you about what strengths they see in you.

- Think about the legacy you would like to leave behind when you pass.

  - What would you like to change or create that will last long after you're gone?

- What knowledge or skills will help you do that?

- What is your purpose?

- What unique traits, qualities, talents, and abilities do you possess?

- What motivates you?

- Now, put it all together and write your personal mission statements.

Chasing Away The Blues

Regardless of how happy you are, how successful you are, or how smoothly life is going, you will occasionally feel down. You need to have resources at your disposal to combat the blues when they start to set in.

Whatever it is, as long as it suits you well, is all that matters. It might be taking a nap, writing, exercising, lifting weights, taking a bubble bath, reading a book, or playing video games.

Everyone needs to engage in something that lifts their spirits, relaxes their minds, and provides them a boost. To continue on your path of growth, you must overcome these moods as part of your personal development journey.

Hobbies can improve your mental health and relieve stress, which will also contribute to improved mental health.

☐ Make a list of all the pastimes or pursuits that you enjoy. the activities that you waste time on. When you begin to paint, do you forget to eat? When you read, play Sims, or cross stitch, does time pass quickly?

☐ Although you don't need to give it much thought, it's always a good idea to know which activity to use in which situation. For instance, you could prefer a thoughtless rom-com over a novel if you've had a difficult day and are feeling teary. If you've been glued to a screen all day, gardening might be more appealing to you than cross-stitching.

☐ Create a guide if you frequently feel overwhelmed or find it difficult to think properly when you're down. List the types of activities and tasks that assist you get out of a funk and the moods you encounter the most frequently.

You can then quickly identify what would be useful.

Journal

A great tool for personal growth is journaling. You get the chance to express yourself, to explain your views and thinking, and it also serves as a written account of the significant events in your life. You can boost your mood and manage your anxiety and depression symptoms by keeping a journal. It assists you in delegating importance to your worries, fears, and issues, keeps track of any symptoms you might be having, and reduces stress.

You can find out what is causing your stress, worry, or upset in your life by using a notebook to assist you identify stressors. You may take action to address such concerns after you have a clearer understanding of what is happening in your life.

A tried-and-true method of improving your self-care is journaling. It is the advice offered to people all around the world to help you become more aware of your thoughts. You will have a reason, which will help you to accomplish more of your goals, if you keep track of your thoughts, pay attention to your feelings, and evaluate your actions in relation to the outcomes in all areas of your life. I love keeping journals; it has greatly benefited me greatly over the years.

Overall, journaling can aid in self-care by providing a safe space for emotional expression, enhancing self-awareness, facilitating problem-solving, promoting gratitude and positivity, and reducing stress and anxiety. It can be a powerful tool for maintaining and improving your physical, emotional, and mental health.

Brings Focus to the Positives

They claim that what you put your attention on expands and grows more quickly than what you ignore. So, pay attention and make a note of the nice and positive things in your life at least once every day if you want your life to feel happier and be more successful. Journaling provides a safe space to express emotions: Journaling provides a safe and private space to express your emotions and thoughts without fear of judgment. It can help you release negative emotions and process difficult experiences, leading to emotional catharsis and stress reduction.

Promotes Brain Processing

Even though you don't want to spend the rest of your life dwelling on the bad, you do want to give yourself some time to process your feelings and let go of the bad things that have happened in your life. This will provide you the ability to respond in a way that helps you comprehend what occurred and take the necessary steps for the future. Journaling can help you brainstorm solutions to problems and challenges you face. It can help you organize your thoughts and ideas, leading to more effective problem-solving and decision-making.

Define Your Ideas

Your ideas are little bits of knowledge you collect during your life, like parts of a picture puzzle. On occasion, you may have too much information in your head for your thoughts to make sense. This is due to the incompatibility of some ideas. To be precise, consider the first idea and rephrase it in a different manner. Use concise, lucid information to convey your ideas.

Control Your Emotions

Emotions can be problematic because they occasionally spiral out of control. Don't allow your feelings to dictate what you do. Instead, work on controlling your emotions by reevaluating the circumstance and altering your perception of it. This enables you to alter your emotional response to something suitable, safe, and healthy. Journaling can help you release pent-up emotions and reduce stress and anxiety. It can also help you gain perspective on stressful situations and reduce the impact they have on your overall well-being.

Discover Your Why

Before you accomplish anything in life, you should ask yourself, "Why?" What motivates you to accomplish it? Why do you proceed in this manner? What information led you to make this decision? You can learn more about yourself and the reasons behind your actions by putting your questions, concerns, feelings, and ideas down on paper. Journaling can help you brainstorm solutions to problems and challenges you face. It can help you organize your thoughts and ideas, leading to more effective problem-solving and decision-making.

Allows you to show gratitude

You will be happier and more optimistic in life if you show your thanks more often. It's fascinating how these positive emotions influence everything you do and compound on one another. However, your appreciation increases even more when you concentrate on finding something positive in everyone and everything. Journaling can help you release pent-up emotions and reduce stress and anxiety. It can also help you gain perspective on stressful situations and reduce the impact they have on your overall well-being.

Follows Your Development

You may monitor your success in every area of your life by keeping a notebook. If you don't keep a record in your diary, you might not notice illness symptoms or evidence of your improvement. However, you can review your entries to find out.

Strengthens Your Recall

If you don't give your brain enough time to arrange and refresh your memories, they won't become permanent. Journaling about everything is a great approach to improving your memory. You are more likely to recall what you wrote on your paper if you manually record your thoughts, concepts, and experiences.

Increases Self-Belief

You'll begin to feel more self-assured as you reflect on your life in your notebook. The important factor is that your actions are deliberate. Rather than just responding to events as they arise, you act with purpose. Journaling can help you focus on the positive aspects of your life, fostering gratitude and positive emotions. It can help you appreciate the small things in life and cultivate a more optimistic outlook.

By nurturing yourself in a trackable way through journaling, you may recognize your effective actions and outcomes in every area of your life. As you keep a journal, you'll remember and desire to keep a journal more frequently for your own health and well-being.

☐ To get the most from journaling, you should aim to write daily. You should be keeping a calendar with a schedule of your time so be sure to add this task. The more regularly journal the easier it will get and the more beneficial it will be.

☐ In a perfect world, you would keep a pen and pad of paper handy in case you want to jot your thoughts down. Failing that, use the notepad in your journal.

☐ You don't need to follow any specific structure or outline in keeping your journal. Your journal is a private place for you to create, discuss, record, or do *whatever* you want to do to express your feelings. Don't get caught up worrying about what you're writing, just let it flow, even if you sometimes only feel like doodling.

☐   You don't have to share your journal with others, but you might want to share certain parts with someone close to you. It's up to you to use it as you see it. The purpose of your journal is to find order in the chaos. It's a place to get to know yourself as you uncover your most private feelings, fears, and thoughts.

Set A Monthly Reading Goal

Reading can be used for development, enjoyment, and learning. It's an excellent opportunity for self-education as well as a way to learn, mature, and improve personally. Reading is enjoyable, it can help you learn more about a topic you're interested in, and it can help you escape the tension of your day.

You ought to select a monthly reading objective. You can set your minimum goal at one book each month and, if it helps, break it down into a daily objective since I don't want this to stress you out.

Along with the advantages already mentioned, reading enhances brain connectivity, increases comprehension, expands vocabulary, fosters empathy, lessens stress, lowers blood pressure and pulse rate, and aids in the prevention of cognitive decline.

☐ Start by writing out a list of books you are interested in reading. You can organize them into categories of pleasure, development, and learning. You know your schedule better than anyone and you have a better idea of what times are most stressful. For the stressful periods, aim to read for pleasure, and for those lighter times, you can focus on learning and development.

☐ If you find it difficult to commit, block off time on your calendar for reading. It's also beneficial if you have a calm, cozy place to curl up and read. It's up to you whether you want to block off a chapter or a certain amount of time.

☐ Take out a highlighter and write notes on what you read without hesitation. Making notes or underlining passages that you want to remember will help them stay in your memory.

 Once you get into the habit of reading one book per month, push yourself to read another one. If that seems like too much of a commitment, spread it out by reading three books over the course of two months.

Early To Rise

To be honest, I have a hard time with this one. According to the proverb, "the early bird gets the worm," but in actuality, rising early each morning is a beneficial habit to establish. Since this is a foundational idea for the next, it will be related to it. There are only so many hours in a day, so if you want to maximize them, you must adhere to a strict plan. To make every second count, you must be consistent with your rising time in addition to maintaining a well-organized calendar. It's challenging to fit everything in, but it's simpler if you have a regular wakeup time and make it early.

An early start improves your concentration and productivity. As you accomplish more, your mood and diet will also improve. If you wake up earlier, you'll discover that you have more time to eat a proper breakfast, which will make it easier for you to resist the temptation of the vending machines, fast food restaurants, and gas station food along your route.

You might even observe a change in the condition of your skin. Getting up earlier has some positive effects on your emotions as well. You'll get better sleep, and you'll have more time to indulge in your interests.
There are plenty of people who brag about how little they sleep because they have more time for work, but I want you to have time for the fun stuff too.

- Set your alarm clock five minutes earlier each day until you are able to complete the morning routine you develop in the next paragraph before waking up. Try one minute at a time if five minutes proves to be too difficult for you. The important thing is to rise when your alarm goes off. We rely on too many alarms to get us out of bed. You ought to finish the sentence!

Your Morning Routine

Plan out your morning schedule now. This is your morning routine, and it involves setting priorities based on what is important to you. What's crucial? If you take charge of your day early and get your goals done, it won't be able to get away from you. What does that appear to you to be? What do you wish your morning had been like when you rushed off to work and were already stressed? You should base your regimen around that. Exercise, prayer or meditation, journaling, or simply taking the time to enjoy breakfast, read the newspaper, and pack a lunch for the day are all good examples.

[] This is your chance to decide precisely when you should wake up, building on the earlier advice to get up early. You need to first make a rough sketch of your morning schedule before you can do that. You should allow plenty of time for it, as well as for showering, dressing, and taking care of any other morning-related tasks.

[] What kind of morning habit do you want to have? Write it out.

[] You can follow a shortened version of your morning routine until you are waking up when you want to. Start by completing the component of it that is most crucial to you and that you cherish most. You'll start to reap the benefits as you grow used to this habit and find it easier to wake up a little earlier each morning. You'll eventually notice that you can complete your daily tasks without having to struggle to get out of bed. Your objective is to achieve that.

☐ An example of a morning routine would be to get up as soon as your alarm goes off, get a drink of water, take a shower, put on clothes, and start your tasks. An easy beginning is a good beginning.

Digital Notes

There are several other digital notebooks that you can utilize, including OneNote, Evernote, ProofHub, Notejoy, and Hive. While some of them require a subscription, others provide a free trial first. This is for your personal growth, and if you can afford to pay for it, you should because it will greatly simplify your life. What is the purpose? There are many causes, chief among them being paper slips lost. When you jot down thoughts wherever you can, you accumulate a ton of jumbled notes that you can't make sense of when you later come across them. You may organize everything with the use of digital notes, making management simpler and your life less hectic.

☐ Choose the digital notebook that you prefer, download it to your phone, set up your online account, and sync it to all of your devices so you have it whenever you need it. If you aren't sure which one to choose, then try the free trial the subscription ones offer. Play around with them until you know which one works best for you.

- ☐ Make a note of anything you want to remember, whether it's a specific podcast episode, a quote from a podcast episode, a book you read, or even songs you want to remember for later. You can download the app directly to your phone so it's on your person at all times.

- ☐ It isn't just for quotes, personal development notes, or things along those lines. You can also just use it as your place to keep all of your notes. Many of these apps allow you to add documents, audio, text, scans, and images as well. So, you really can use it for everything, including keeping your schedule.

- ☐ Now use it moving forward and enjoy the organization!

Developmental Media

Podcasts, blogs, books, and more. Whatever your favorite method of material and media consumption, personal growth will be on the menu. Personal development is a big issue.

You can listen to podcasts while driving, cleaning the house, or cooking, which makes them a terrific option. The correct kind of multitasking is being done. The majority of the episodes of The Gary Vee Audio Experience are around 30 minutes long, while some are longer. It is updated every day.

Another great podcast with fewer episodes is The Growth Mindset Podcast, although it only releases new content once each week. These are merely two examples; depending on your particular objectives, a fast online search will turn up an unlimited array of podcasts for you to sample.

If listening to podcasts isn't your thing, try reading or listening to a personal development book or finding a blog that speaks to you. The purpose of this material is to make you think critically. Isn't that what personal development is all about?

You should feel challenged and motivated to act by whatever media or content you consume about personal growth.

☐ Investigate the world of media for personal development right away. Do you have a preferred medium among the others? If yes, where should you begin?

☐ To start your trip, pick five titles (whether they be books, podcasts, or blogs) and focus on one at a time.

☐ Once you've chosen the material you prefer, schedule it in your daily calendar.

☐ Review your media intake frequently. This is not to argue that you can't listen to things for pleasure's sake. The key is to ensure that the personal development material you select challenges you. If it reaches a point where you no longer feel challenged, you should move on to something else.

Give Generously

Giving and helping others has a double impact. You become happier as a result, and it also has a favorable effect on the rest of the world. In case the joy wasn't enough to persuade you, giving can help increase self-esteem, lessen depressive symptoms, combat stress, and eventually lengthen your life. It certainly does sound like a good deal, especially when you take into account all the many options there are to donate.

☐ It's not necessary to be wealthy to contribute generously. If you can, start by allocating a certain portion of your income to a charity or cause that is important to you.

☐ Even if you don't have a lot of money, you can still donate generously by doing this. The secret is to give consistently and to pick a cause that is close to your heart. Make sure the charity or cause you chose sends the funds where they say they will by checking twice.

☐ If you are unable to consistently provide money, there is one resource that is considerably more precious than cash: your time. It's possibly your most valuable possession, making it a unique chance to give back.

☐ Do you possess any unique talents? Your community will benefit from your application of these abilities. Do you excel in math?

Why not offer tutoring at the neighborhood community center? Are you an avid gardener?

Why not spend some time organizing a gardening crew in your town or neighborhood? Are you a sports fan?

▢ You can coach minor league, iron on patches, stitch jerseys, or you can just give oranges at halftime.

▢ You might not think of blood donation as giving, but it is. You never know whose life you will save by donating blood regularly.

▢ If you have an elderly neighbor or someone struggling by on their own, you can offer to run errands and pick up shopping for them. Even sitting for a chat and a cup of coffee with them is a help.

The Gratitude Jar

A gratitude jar is a great concept because it only only a few seconds of daily effort but has a significant impact. Create a brief letter to place once each day in the jar. Thank someone for something that happened that day. Writing it down will serve as a constant reminder of your good fortune. You can look back on all of these little messages you have written to yourself at the end of the year and be reminded once more of how fortunate you are.

The more gratitude you express, the happier you'll feel. The benefits don't end there; you'll also start to attract more positivity and generally feel more upbeat.

There is evidence that gratitude might help lessen the signs and symptoms of anxiety and sadness. Gratitude has several unanticipated advantages, such as enhanced connections, tighter ties, and increased social support.

- Start by choosing a jar or box large enough to house 365 notes. If you want to involve your family, then you will need an even bigger jar/box! If you do involve your family gives everyone a specific color of pen and paper to use so the different notes are easily identifiable.
- For instance, you could write on a blue sticky note with a black pen, your partner could write on a yellow sticky note with a blue pen, etc. The various colored papers will provide some interest if your container is translucent.
- You can make the reading of the box a New Year's Eve tradition if you decide to include your family.

Naturally, it would take a while to get through them all, so let's each choose a few to read aloud before everyone goes their separate ways to finish them before the new year begins.

Improve Your Relationships

You spend a lot of time with your coworkers, therefore it shouldn't need to be mentioned how crucial it is to get along with them. In addition to spending more time with them than your family, cooperation is essential for success in practically every sector of business and workplace worldwide.

For the sake of the job, it's crucial that you get along with everyone you work with, even if they don't all have to like you. Because you are all adults, you should be able to set aside any tension and focus on the task at hand.

Establishing solid working relationships is a crucial aspect of building a successful future. Everyone, whether directly or indirectly, contributes to your performance and success.

You will get stronger if you nurture these bonds. It will advance not just your career but also make work simpler and more pleasurable. You will develop your interpersonal relationships, gain trust, and reduce stress as a result.

☐ Start developing better business relationships by adopting a positive work style. It will increase your job happiness and assist you in forging stronger bonds with your coworkers. Be receptive to fresh ideas and listen when someone offers them.

☐ Consider a diversity of viewpoints when making decisions, and keep in mind that everyone has something to contribute. You'll have better relationships with others if they realize that you value them and their opinions.

☐ If you have the time, you could suggest meeting up with some of your colleagues outside of work. It's always nice to grab drinks and get to know people on a personal level.

Practice Time Management

How can you find the time to complete everything when one deadline will be interrupted for a more significant deadline in addition to your regular day job? Of course, time management!

There are things that need your time and attention, and those needs will never go away. It could occasionally feel unattainable, which is why it's crucial that you have efficient time management skills.

Time management will not only guarantee that you have enough time to do everything, but it will also lower your stress levels and boost your productivity. You'll have plenty of time for other things once you're proficient at managing your time.How can you find the time to complete everything when one deadline will be interrupted for a more significant deadline in addition to your regular day job? Of course, time management!

There are things that need your time and attention, and those needs will never go away. It could occasionally feel unattainable, which is why it's crucial that you have efficient time management skills.

Time management will not only guarantee that you have enough time to do everything, but it will also lower your stress levels and boost your productivity.

You'll have plenty of time for other things once you're proficient at managing your time.

To become a proficient time manager, you must work on three distinct talents. First, be conscious of the fact that time is a finite resource, thus estimate task durations accurately. The second skill is the capacity for smart and sensible organization of your objectives, plans, and tasks. The capacity to keep track of your time and adjust as necessary if priorities shift. Examining the appropriate approach will help us.

- You need to start paying attention to how you spend your time. If necessary, use a diary or app to do so.

- When you write your to-do list or create your schedule, assign each task a specific amount of time to complete it. In these time zones, distractions are not allowed. Your sole focus should be on said task.

- How do you give each task a certain amount of time? You can monitor how long it takes you to complete each of your everyday duties for a week or two. This will be an essential and eye-opening experience.

- Always prioritize your most important chores first, and then fit everything else into your calendar.

- Have a fallback strategy

Work On Your Emotional Intelligence

Compared to IQ, emotional intelligence is a much better indicator of success. A high IQ alone won't get you very far; but, a high EQ combined with an ordinary IQ will take you far. How is a high EQ beneficial?

First of all, it gives you the tools you need to understand your own and other people's feelings better. It's simpler to relate to people when one has a better understanding of their emotions, making it a powerful skill. Your communication abilities and social skills will both increase as a result.

All people have emotions, although not everyone is aware of the particular feelings they are feeling at any one time. A person with a high EQ will be able to recognize that the terrible feeling is annoyance, grief, or hurt, whereas a person with a low EQ may just state that they are feeling lousy.

Your ability to characterize an emotion precisely will increase your understanding of its root causes and, consequently, your ability to resolve the problem.

All people have emotions, although not everyone is aware of the particular feelings they are feeling at any one time. A person with a high EQ will be able to recognize that the terrible feeling is annoyance, grief, or hurt, whereas a person with a low EQ may just state that they are feeling lousy. The more precisely you

☐ Self-awareness is perhaps the most crucial component of developing emotional intelligence. If you are really conscious of who you are, it is much simpler to comprehend what you are feeling. Create a mindfulness diary to begin the process of developing self-awareness. Daily journaling will help you develop the habit of living in the now and become more conscious of your surroundings and self. You can start developing your social awareness after your self-awareness is better.

☐ Self-control is essential since it's simple to lose control while you're experiencing strong emotions, but doing so isn't a good idea. Your emotions are indicators; they provide insight into who you are, and as you observe and experience the emotions of others, you learn more about them. Gaining control of your emotions begins with managing your stress levels.

☐ Relationship management is another crucial component of emotional intelligence since it directly affects the kinds of connections you make and keep with others around you. Because your body language should match your words, pay attention to how you express yourself nonverbally.

Define Success

Find out what success means to some of your neighbors. You'll probably get a range of responses, but a lot of them will be about money or a title. That does not imply that you must define success in that manner.

Finding happiness can be your idea of success, and taking the necessary steps to accomplish so will be the first step you take toward realizing your success. I contend that those who define success in terms of a job title or a salary lack a clear understanding of their beliefs or their life's purpose.

You'll stop seeking success in the ways that other people perceive it once you have a greater grasp of it.

☐ You must first identify your basic values before you can define success. By realizing there is no one like you, you will understand that you cannot compare yourself to others. What other people do does not alter your aspirations in life, and the accomplishment of another person's aim does not preclude your own.

☐ So what exactly defines you as who you are? What distinguishing traits do you possess? You should have an easier time understanding this phase if you think back to your personal mission statement.

☐ Do what it takes to be your best self and challenge limiting beliefs. Make sure you are engaging in self-care because that calls for it.

Find A New Challenge

You will undoubtedly suffer if you have been at your career for a while or if it is a job you don't particularly enjoy. If your career no longer feels satisfying or exciting to you, you should look for a new challenge. This kind of personal development objective focuses on your aspirations and conveys to your employers that you are committed to and ambitious for the organization. It also gives you something enjoyable to do at work, which is more crucial. It doesn't have to be anything outrageous; it could simply include updating a manual that hasn't changed since the 1990s.

A new challenge will highlight your leadership skills and help you progress as a person and in your career.

☐ First things first: discuss your current tasks with your manager. If you don't know what new task you can accept, take advantage of this situation to ask your supervisor what projects you can assist with. That might result in career advancement, which would present a unique problem.

☐ By concentrating on yourself, you can also discover new difficulties. Your professional advancement doesn't necessarily have to revolve around pleasing your boss. That ought to be a beneficial outcome of looking for new difficulties, but it shouldn't be the primary one.

☐ Finding fulfillment is the whole objective of a new challenge, thus you must take yourself into account. You will start to get sluggish and disinterested in your work if you fall into the trap of working for someone else. Your work will be much better if you keep in mind that it is a reflection of you and not of your employer.

No Passivity

Why does that matter? It implies that you become a passive person when you prioritize the wants or needs of others before your own. Although passive behavior is a great tool for fostering connections, it can be risky if it persists over time. There will come a time when it becomes an obstacle to your achievement. Conflict avoiders frequently act in a passive manner. Do you let things happen without putting out a reasoned defense or defending yourself? If so, others may perceive your passivity as a desire to please them, which gives them the opportunity to take advantage of you.

Passivity for a short period of time can be an effective strategy for winning others over to your point of view. Long-term passivity, however, is harmful since the longer it persists, the more people will expect of you, necessitating greater sacrifices in order to sustain those connections.

☐ Write a career goal statement if you wish to approach your career in a proactive manner. Similar to the goal statement you created for your life, but focused only on your profession. This is done to help you clearly see what you want out of your work life and to lay out the specific steps you need to take to get there.

☐ Engaging directly with people is a great approach to avoid developing a passive attitude. If you're timid, this might be difficult, but once you get into the practice of speaking directly to people, it shouldn't take long. Learn how to be assertive without coming out as aggressive by being sincere, straightforward, and assertive. When you're just getting acclimated to being an assertive person after being passive for so long, it's easy to cross the line.

Develop a Growth Mindset

An individual with a development mentality thinks they can and will continue to progress throughout their life. People with a growth mindset typically accomplish more than those with a fixed perspective. The latter think they can only use the skills they were born with; they don't think they can learn new ones. They spend little time or effort developing since they are content with who they are. In contrast, a growth mentality encourages people to constantly work on themselves.

Someone with a development mentality is willing to collaborate, shares information, strives to improve, accepts responsibility for mistakes, and asks for criticism in a professional setting.

A fixed mindset, on the other hand, is risk-averse. They are afraid of stepping outside of their comfort zone for fear that they will fail or look foolish if they do. Although you may think that is wise, a locked perspective prevents you from moving forward.

They miss out on so much by avoiding opportunities. The good news is that you can change your perspective to one of progress even if you now have a stuck mindset. Every element of your life benefits from a growth attitude, but your work benefits the most.

- We have already touched on the importance of self-awareness in developing a growth mindset, so ideally you are already on that path.

- Recognize and accept your flaws rather than avoiding them because those are your opportunities and that's where your personal growth may achieve great success. A key part of developing a growth mindset is realizing them and thinking that you can become better.

- Both your strengths and your weaknesses present opportunities. It's not meant to trip you up; rather, it's meant to test you.

- Failure will no longer exist. It's an opportunity, a learning experience, and a hiccup. You can only fail if you stumble and remain on the ground. You are not failing as long as you continue to get back up.

Grow Your Network

People like to work and socialize with people they know and trust. In the realm of business, it's crucial to keep in mind that individuals, not the firm, decide how things are done. Therefore, developing a strong professional network can aid in job advancement because no one succeeds in their field alone. You never know when new connections you make through networking will be useful because they may have more knowledge and experience. Keep up with building your network since you never know when you'll need assistance or when a chance may present itself that someone will consider you for!

- If you don't put yourself in novel and unpleasant situations, your network won't grow. Attend networking events, bring a friend if you're shy, but once you're there, put yourself out there!
- Take business cards, strike up conversations, and make introductions. As you attend these activities more frequently, you will begin to recognize familiar faces more frequently, which will provide you more opportunities to chat with others.
- Although nothing replaces that face-to-face connection you can make at networking events, social media is still a fantastic tool to expand your network.

Find Your Balance

You must strike the correct balance between work and life if you want to be happy. This means that you must take enough time off from work to rest and recharge, which will improve your general happiness and wellbeing. Your performance and productivity at work will increase as a result of that.

The lines between your personal and professional lives must be drawn clearly and realistically. That could imply that you put in your eight hours and then quit. It could entail leaving your work at the workplace when you finish for the day so that you can focus entirely on your family during the time you spend at home.

In the end, maintaining a healthy balance is about making sure you have a personal life while still being motivated to work hard. You will lose motivation and interest in what work has to offer if you are frequently interrupted by it in your personal life.

☐ You must be productive at work if you want to maintain a balance. If you don't efficiently manage your time, work will start to encroach on your free time. You should talk to your manager about your workload if you are productive yet your workload still overflows. You may be assuming too much.

- Plan your work week so that you may properly manage your time. If you have a plan in place, it is much simpler to accomplish your goals and complete everything effectively. Otherwise, you risk procrastinating because you feel overburdened by the tasks on your list and are unsure of how to proceed.

Don't Be So Serious

I've already told you to enjoy yourself, but this is a little different. It's simple to lose sight of the broad picture when you're focused on the smaller details, but you need to remember it every day.

Most of us have our basic needs met and are healthy, but we lose sight of how fortunate we are when we become preoccupied with unimportant details. Do you know somebody who, despite making a substantial income, becomes quickly irritated, furious, and angered over even the most minor inconveniences?

If you learn to take things less seriously you will be less stressed, far happier, and more enjoyable to be around. There are no greater benefits than that. Laugh when you run into an unexpected challenge or inconvenience, laugh off mistakes, laugh at every opportunity because it makes life better.

- A fantastic place to start is with appreciation since it helps you focus on all the wonderful things in your life. Additionally, being grateful will support you in keeping a happy outlook.

- Another helpful way to avoid taking things too seriously is stress management. It's challenging to unwind and enjoy life when you're carrying around wrath, tension, and anxiety. Therefore, develop stress management skills to prevent them from weighing you down.

Practice Self-Care

If you don't look after yourself, how do you think you will be of use to anyone else? While you don't exist to serve or please others, part of life is the connections that we build with other people.

If you have children you have to be able to look after their needs just as you do your own. The problem is that many people work hard to cater to everyone else's needs without attending to their own and that's an issue.

By practicing self-care, you make your health and happiness a priority and that is going to improve your life greatly. You can't take care of anything else until you take care of yourself.

☐ Find a hobby that you love to do, something you enjoy and makes time fly.

☐ Keep a journal.

☐ Declutter your home and workspace.

☐ Try a creative pursuit, even if it's just an adult coloring book.

☐ When you do positive things, give yourself a reward.

Most experts agree that there are at least eight different aspects of self-care that you should consider. You may maximize each aspect of your life over the course of your lifetime by using the categories listed below. It's crucial to cherish and take care of oneself, just as you would a friend or family member, whether you come from a big family or not.

- **Physical -** To take care of your physical needs, consume wholesome meals and snacks and engage in regular exercise. Also, maintain a minimal level of hygiene. Make time in your schedule to take care of yourself by engaging in physical activities that uplift and revitalize you.
- **Psychological -** Considering that your mind has a significant impact on every aspect of your life, self-care for your mind is crucial. Engage in activities that challenge your mind, such as capturing pictures, playing board games with strategy, and problem-solving exercises. Your mind will live longer and be in better health as you age if you take better care of it today.
- **Emotional -** It's crucial to keep your emotions in good shape throughout your life. You may function more efficiently and keep your personal energy stable by keeping your emotions in check. Using self-care techniques that are specific to your needs, such as deep breathing, embracing your feelings, journaling about your feelings, etc., you can learn to develop, understand, and control your emotions.
- **Social -** When people are deprived of social interactions and connections, particularly as children, it can result in a number of long-term

health problems. To live a happy, healthy, and fulfilling life, it is crucial to incorporate social self-care practices into daily interactions with people and the development of healthy relationships.

- **Professional -** Since it affects both your performance and others around you, workplace self-care frequently includes your physical and emotional wellbeing. It also involves workplace-specific professional development, though. Not only do you suffer when you don't take care of yourself, but your team and the company may suffer as well. Whilst at work, take a few minutes for self-care.

- **Environmental -** Your productivity will increase if you declutter your house, office, and thinking. If you don't clear the clutter, you could experience worry and anxiety, which might cause more serious issues.

- **Spiritual -** Practicing spiritual self-care has a variety of positive effects on one's health. You're more likely to lead a life that is balanced when you engage in some sort of spiritual self-care. Your relationship with your higher self or higher being will strengthen as a result of this kind of self-care. Also, it aids with mood control, wise decision-making, and appreciation of others.

- **Finance -** Individuals who don't take care of their finances often lose or waste money. Financial self-care techniques make you more responsible with your money, which in turn helps you buy and sell more sensibly. You must understand where your money comes from and where it is going when you spend it. This gives you the ability to make wise short-term and long-term goals for yourself. Even though self-care can occasionally seem difficult, only you are capable of knowing your own wants and needs. However, only you have power over your ideas and deeds. You look after yourself better than anyone else as a result.

Be Proactive

If there is one thing that is certain in life, it is that mistakes may and will be made. You have the option of allowing them to be no more than a little annoyance or a significant issue. Whether you are a proactive or a reactive person will probably determine how you respond.

If you react to issues as they happen on a regular basis, they are probably far more distressing. However, if you approach life with a proactive mindset, problems can be easily avoided and you feel more grounded.

You are equipped to face difficulties. Regardless of what could go wrong, you are prepared. The advantage of being proactive is that you always feel like you are in control.

[] The most important signs of proactivity are working to solve problems and concentrating on solutions. It's important to think quickly and be prepared for any situation, not to do everything in advance.

[] Get motivated people around you to boost your chances of success. People close to you may bring you down to their level if they lack motivation. You will stay ahead if you hang around with proactive, driven, and motivated people. You may achieve this by keeping up with the most recent trends and information and keeping an eye on what's happening in your sector.

Increase Your Patience

Being patient can be difficult, especially for people with volatile personalities. But with enough work, you may learn to be more patient. Being patient is a virtue to possess, especially when coping with difficult situations. Keeping your cool will help you solve problems more quickly and without becoming bogged down by frustration.

You will make better decisions as a result of practicing patience, this is fantastic news for your long-term satisfaction. When you rush into decisions, you're more likely to make them, which leads to more effort because you have to rectify things.

☐ Before you decide, pause and give the situation some serious thought. That gives you more time and prevents regret.

☐ Choose a patience-testing activity, such as learning a new language, mastering a difficult recipe, or learning how to play the guitar or piano.

☐ While you wait for something you really want, you can exercise patience by paying attention to your breathing and developing an attitude of thankfulness.

☐ Work on controlling your frustration and anger because impatience often comes with those emotions. This will help you lessen the negative effects of impatience.

Drop Toxicity

Remove the poisonous people from your life, explicitly. I want to be clear about what I mean by toxic people before I go any further. I'm not referring to a friend who is experiencing a difficult time and is more dependent than usual. I'm also not referring to a friend who complains to you and then expects the same in return. Now there's a friendship.

As long as there is reciprocity, friends can vent to one another without it being poisonous. Many folks appear to be confused about the degree of toxicity I'm referring to. The poisonous buddy I'm referring to is the one who continuously disparages you, puts you down, or who is constantly whining and judging everyone in your life.

People who are toxic will always hold you back because they don't want to be passed by. If you associate with these negative people, you will never succeed in your ambitions. It can be difficult to shut out a toxic person who was a childhood friend, but you don't have to; you can just limit how much time you spend with them. The best you can do if there is a toxic individual at work is to avoid them as much as you can.

It's more vital to surround oneself with the correct kind of people rather than just getting rid of poisonous people. You need people to support you and pull you up as well as those who can call you out when it's necessary.

☐ You can't wait for toxic individuals to change because that's not going to happen until they decide to. The best course of action is to set and uphold limits so they can't draw you into their problems.

☐ When they repeatedly step over your established and enforced boundaries, you may want to consider cutting off your relationship. People can and will grow in a variety of ways since we are all growing. Not everybody was intended to stay in your life permanently.

Accept Reality

How well-aware of yourself are you? Your response isn't really important since what's more important is that you accept who you are. Whether you think you've found fulfillment in your work, relationship, or house, your reality is what it is.

Before you can even consider making improvements, you must first accept things as they are. We are all, and always will be, merely works in progress. Until the day we die, we continue to grow or develop (or at least we should). Until you embrace your reality for what it is, you won't move forward.

Even when things are bad, it's still one of the best things you can do for yourself. Accepting and realizing that you have the ability to improve things is the first step.

Finding all of those sources of unhappiness will enable you to start implementing improvements. Otherwise? You'll continue to be unhappy and complacent.

- Even if it takes time to address every negative aspect, doing so is necessary if you want to experience positive outcomes. Accept responsibility for all of it—the good, the bad, and the ugly—for the errors you have made and the part you have played in other problems. How did you encourage failure? How did you achieve success? Please note that this is not a reason to berate yourself. It's a chance to learn something. As you deserve it, be kind to yourself.

Know What Defines You

More importantly, avoid letting your history determine who you are. Many people have regrettable pasts and skeletons in their closets. But we let the weight of the past hang over us like a burden. Your teacher may have left an impression on you that led you to believe that your ambitions will always be just out of reach. Perhaps your first romantic partner broke your heart and left you reeling, leading you to believe that you are unlovable, undeserving, or unworthy. Maybe anything from your past makes you feel uncomfortable. We all have experiences that we wish we could forget or had never happened, so you're not alone in this.

If you performed some investigation, it wouldn't take you long to come across a number of success tales of people who have faced great adversity and overcame it to achieve success.

If they are able to get past their past, you can ensure that yours won't define you. Your past should never stand in the way of achieving your goals; rather, it should serve as a guide for what to do (and what not to do) in the future.

☐ Because it has contributed so much to the formation of your identity, it won't be simple to let go, but it is achievable. You must identify the unpleasant feelings that are a result of your history and consider their origin, occurrence, and management. If you're having trouble figuring it out, you might need to talk to someone.

☐ Once you've discovered your limiting emotions, you can concentrate on positive motivating reasons to go through those emotions. After doing this, you can construct a happy experience to consign those unpleasant thoughts and events to the past, where they belong. You'll have the time and space necessary to design the contented, joyful life you deserve as a result.

Let Go of Beliefs That Limit You

You are infinite, and if you continue to hold onto limiting notions, you will never venture beyond of your comfort zone. People who are enslaved by restricting beliefs are unable to take chances, try new things, or mature and evolve as humans are meant to. The fear of failure is one justification people frequently provide for staying in their comfort zones. If that isn't the case, they can be afraid of getting wounded. Although those are legitimate emotions, they are insufficient to keep you where you are. Fear of failing and fear of being harmed are obstacles to overcome, not justifications for staying in one's current position.

You can pursue improvement by letting rid of these notions. A limiting belief is what? It could be about your skill level, relationships, finances, work-related issues, or even friendships. To succeed, you must recognize all of the ideas that are preventing you from moving forward and devise strategies to not only dispel them but also to remove them.

☐ Finding out what your limiting ideas are and then challenging them with empowering thoughts are the first two steps to conquering them.

☐ Continually testing your beliefs to see if they serve you or not will help you with both of the aforementioned phases. If the response is no, you can consider if those ideas are accurate, whether there is evidence to support them, or whether you are engaging in black-and-white thinking.

☐ You must be ready to be brutally honest with yourself about your way of thinking and your beliefs. You'll have to think creatively, but you might find it enjoyable.

Establish Boundaries

Many people find it difficult to say no to requests. At work, you want to be liked by your coworkers and respected by your supervisor for your dependability and diligence. In your private life, you want people to be able to count on you, to call you for assistance, and to consider you a trustworthy friend.

The issue is that if you never say no, even when you want to, it becomes impossible. There is only one way for you to change how people see you because you are currently seen as an unending resource: by setting (and upholding) boundaries.

Your boundaries are unique to you. Only you know where your limits are since only you manage your calendar and keep track of your time and energy consumption. So establish boundaries and uphold them! Boundaries at work, relationships with family, or even your love partner could be the cause.

Establishing mutually respectful and supportive partnerships requires having clear limits. If you don't set limits, you'll leave yourself up to exploitation or being taken for granted by others.

- ☐ Setting boundaries requires sitting down and identifying your strict limitations, which you must accomplish as the first step.

- ☐ Self-awareness is crucial since it will enable you to identify those who are stepping over your boundaries. When you see this kind of boundary-pushing or -crossing, you may put your foot down without feeling bad if you have a healthy sense of self-respect.

- ☐ Start simple by telling your family and friends that your phone will be put on quiet every night at 7:30 and won't be touched again until your alarm goes off at 6:30 in the morning. This is about developing time-boundary awareness. From there, you can decide that you won't check your email after work.

Learn How To Actively Listen

Every day, you converse with a variety of people, but how attentively do you listen? You undoubtedly believe that you are an exceptional communicator and listener, but research indicates that this may not be the truth.

In fact, according to the Harvard Business Review (https://hbr.org/1957/09/listening-to-people), specialists estimate that we only retain about 25% of what we hear.

If you spend half of a 20-minute conversation with friends, family, coworkers, or your boss talking, they will only retain around 2.5 minutes of your conversation when they leave. You are likely to miss a lot of what someone is saying when they are telling you crucial information.

Everyone could use the ability of active listening, and we can all gain from it. Your capacity to convince and negotiate, as well as your productivity and ability to influence people, can all be improved as you hone these talents.

In addition to being clear speakers, great communicators are also great listeners. Active listening demonstrates your concern, empathy, and support for your communication partner, which will benefit you.

☐ Body language is a crucial component in communicating to people that you are actively participating in the conversation. You can demonstrate your interest and make sure you comprehend the message they are conveying by imitating their actions and, where appropriate, asking questions. You can take the chance to repeat their message back to them to make sure you are understanding it correctly and to let them know you are actually listening by nodding in agreement and showing that you are interested in what they are saying.

☐ Make an effort to keep comfortable eye contact.

☐ Never be reluctant to ask follow-up or clarifying questions because doing so demonstrates your attention and engagement.

Learn How To Let Go

It will be far more challenging to become your true self and the person you wish to be if you persist on clinging to your past. Life is simpler when you let go of everything, but it is much easier said than done.

It's fair to say, in my opinion, that when someone offers to "just let it go," a bull sees it as a red rag. It doesn't convince you to let go; if anything, it makes you even angrier and more upset than you were before. Since the pain from the past has been with you for such a long time and is now a part of who you are, it is tough to let go of it.

If those terrible experiences and painful memories stick with you, they will only be a burden on your shoulders and prevent you from living a full life.

In order to move on with the lessons you learned from those experiences, you must work through your emotions and let go of the hurt and negativity. Release the emotional burden, but hold on to the lessons you've learnt.

- To let go, forgiveness is a crucial component. It doesn't imply you forget about the hurt someone gave you; it just means you won't let it affect you negatively any longer. In order to heal from your suffering, you must forgive, not in order to clear the other person of wrongdoing.

□   You'd do well to keep in mind that you are in charge of your thoughts and deeds. Therefore, don't waste time or effort trying to control other people. You shouldn't be concerned by their opinions any more than they should be. Being the best version of yourself and leading the life you've imagined should be your main priorities.

Build Your Resilience Levels

Even the most self-aware people might be surprised by life's difficulties, which is why it's crucial to increase your resilience. You will recover more quickly if you learn how to handle difficult situations in a healthy way, which should speed up your progress.

You can deal with adversity and adjust when things don't go your way if you have resilience. Being resilient can make the difference between facing challenges head-on and disintegrating at the first indication of difficulty. When you bounce back swiftly, you do so more powerfully.

Resilience will enable you to deal with whatever is thrown your way. Resilience is a skill you can develop that can help you in all aspects of your life and make any challenge appear more doable.

- You cannot intentionally seek out difficulty in order to develop resilience; yet, the more hardship you experience, the more likely you are to do so. You must take chances since doing so increases your likelihood of failing, and failing is the whetstone that sharpens your blade. It's crucial to always keep in mind that failure, however difficult it may be to accept, is never the end of a journey; rather, it is merely a little diversion with a lesson along the road.

- A common tool used by persons trying to develop resilience is journaling. In addition to being a practical tool to explore your ideas, keeping a journal can help you arrange and organize your ideas. That can give you a fresh viewpoint on your earlier encounters. You can organize your thoughts and feelings in a notebook, for instance, if your relationship is going through a challenging time. By doing this, you can find that you missed your partner's point entirely while trying to make your own.

Deliver Solutions

Do you frequently point up issues? You might believe that by presenting problems after problems without offering solutions, you are helping others, but in reality, you are bothering them.

I want you to imagine how it would feel if someone constantly called your attention to your problems without ever coming up with a single solution. That sounds like it would be a lot of work. You need to be proactive and identify an issue while providing a solution. You can't keep pointing out problems after problems.

What would you do, for instance, if your coworker kept writing reports incorrectly and you had to go back and amend them all the time? You run the risk of sounding whiny if you bring up the matter with your supervisor directly. In contrast, you are solving issues if you approach a coworker to ask if they need assistance or if they are having a problem.

☐ If you aren't seeking for solutions to your problems, what good is it to sit around and talk about them? Have an open and sincere discussion with those concerned to try and find a solution, whatever the circumstance. Include your own answer if you have one handy. In that case, you can demonstrate your labor if the situation worsens.

☐ Using the previous scenario once again, if you have helped your colleague and provided remedies yet the errors continue, you should speak with your employer. When you do, though, you can emphasize the actions you took to resolve the problem. It's not about assigning blame.

Expect Change

Since change is the one constant in life, you must have flexibility and the ability to accept change when it occurs. Whether it be in interpersonal interactions, friendships, or the profession, the world is continuously changing.

If you can't keep up with the rapid advancements made by humans, you'll fall behind. As a result, you must always be ready to change, flex, and adapt. It will be much simpler if you think of yourself as a perpetual learner.

☐ Knowledge is the basis for flexibility and adaptability, thus you should increase your knowledge if you want to become more adept at foreseeing prospective change. This could entail keeping up with the latest developments in your field or paying more attention to your spouse's body language and other nonverbal clues. There will always be disturbance, but you get to choose how you react to it.

☐ Look for books and courses on a topic in your life that you are aware is prone to change. Because anything can happen, be ready for anything.

Learn to Manage People

Even though you might just think of this as a talent for the office, understanding people management techniques can help you grow personally. Whether you hold a leadership position or not, setting a good example for others will help you manage them.

When you act as a team player in front of others, it inspires them to do the same. Being influential can happen without having a formal title or position, and that is what people management is all about.

Being an effective communicator and performer will serve you well no matter what your future ambitions may be. You can discover new abilities and areas of yourself to grow by developing the management skills necessary to manage others. The advantages are innumerable.

- You can use your people management abilities by demonstrating sympathy to your coworkers while they are going through trying times, whether at work or in their personal lives. You can put yourself in their situation and consider what they might be going through.

- If there is a problem, you can follow up to support those ideas and potential remedies by providing feedback that is both positive and helpful.

- You can tell when your coworkers go above and beyond the call of duty.

- Create a welcoming environment where everyone's ideas and opinions are welcomed.

Make Confident Decisions

You need to have faith in the choices you make, and if you stop to think about how many decisions you make each day, you'll see how frequently you get the chance to practice making snap decisions. If you consider all of the choices you make each day, you can easily determine if they had favorable or unfavorable effects. More positivity is what you want from your decisions, but getting there requires having the ability to swiftly analyze a scenario.

By improving your decision-making abilities, you can enhance the likelihood of successful results while lowering the possibility of costly errors.

Before you get carried away, be aware that this talent has a learning curve and that you will make mistakes. The important thing is to learn from them so that you can make better decisions in the future.

- Limiting your alternatives will help you make better selections. You will simply feel overwhelmed if there are too many options, so eliminate as many as you can.
- Never undervalue the influence of making a list of advantages and disadvantages before choosing a course of action. It will assist you in finding any buried issues or details.
- Set a deadline for making your choice. It was enough to think about something while you

slept; you didn't need to obsess over it for 10 days.

Any choice you make, do your homework. It can entail checking out reviews, getting in touch with acquaintances, or conducting online research. There is always research to be done, regardless of your choice.

Speak Out

An engaging and clear public speaker exudes confidence. Even if you aren't necessarily a public speaker, it's a useful ability to have. It's a topic that frequently arises in the job, so you should brush up on it so you are ready when the time comes. It may happen in just about every aspect of life, including team leaders informing their teams, salespeople making presentations, and executives making a board presentation.

While there are several advantages, the most obvious advantage is the ability to talk to a crowd of people at any time. Another advantage is that you'll experience less worry and trepidation about speaking in front of a crowd.

- Consider joining a group that focuses on helping you develop your public speaking abilities.

- To improve your public speaking abilities, enroll in a class.

- Before speaking to a formal audience, practice speaking clearly and confidently in front of a mirror. Once you feel more at ease, you can also practice with friends and family.

Live With Intention

Why don't you start living with intention instead of just wishing for something or hoping against hope that it would come true? Although you can utilize intention in any area of your life, it is undoubtedly simpler to see results faster in a romantic setting. Let's say you recently became single and run across an old acquaintance. You start to think, "I hope it works out." Instead of wishing it would happen, take action and make it happen! Consider how you might ask for a raise instead of expecting for a promotion.

- Forget about outside influences, circumstances, fate, or other people's perceptions. Instead, take charge of your life by living with a purpose and an intention to direct it in the direction you desire. You are the author of your life as well as the major character.

▢ If you catch yourself hoping and longing for something, tell yourself that you can and will make them come true.

Track Your Moods

Please be patient with me because, although we've talked about concepts like this before, this one stands alone. You can jot down a brief entry each day tracking your mood in the diary you should already be keeping (s). Although it may seem insignificant, being aware of your moods is an excellent way to improve your self-awareness. In addition, it is a chore that will assist you in being aware of the things, people, and occasions that affect your mood. You should not only learn to control your emotions and stop letting other people affect them, but you should also learn how to handle events that have the potential to affect your mood.

▢ Reflect every week so you may organize the following week accordingly. You can write out the emotion itself or use a color-coded system if it makes things easier.

Conquer Fear

Fear is one of the major impediments to growth. If there is one thing that will stop you from growing and moving forward in life, it is fear. We just discussed how your fear of failure is holding you back, but there are many more concerns that could be doing the same.

A mentor can boost your self-esteem and motivate you to take wiser decisions. You can learn to cope with anxiety and discomfort by forcing yourself into uncomfortable situations.

You can only truly learn and develop by putting yourself in uncomfortable situations. Your growth is dependent upon it.

- Take a break to calm yourself down if your fear makes you feel threatened. Breathe through the fear.

- Consider the worst-case scenario. Why are you so afraid of this? Once you speak it out loud, even the worst worst-case scenario starts to seem silly.

- Forget about imperfection; if you keep striving to reach it, you'll go insane.

- Imagine yourself in a happy, secure location as you sit down. When you experience excessive dread, worry, or panic, close your eyes and transport yourself to your most vivid image of happiness.

- Rewarding oneself is important when you face a fear or put yourself out there.

Move At Your Own Speed

No matter what you are working on or trying to achieve, you can only do so at your own pace. No one else can push you further than you are willing to go since you control the pace for your development. Similarly, if you establish your own pace, nobody can slow you down. There is always a chance that you will burn out from overcommitting or lose interest from under committing.

Be fair to yourself if you miss a deadline after setting one and then proceed at your own pace.

Being merely human, you shouldn't always push yourself to achieve achievements because occasionally life gets in the way. It's usually a good idea to constantly assess your progress so you can adjust your timeline as necessary. That may seem paradoxical, but the key is to control expectations and maintain reality.

If you are too hard on yourself you will knock your confidence, derail your motivation, and ultimately, you will lose track of the goal. The best way to overcome this? Write your goals out and create a detailed plan of how you plan to achieve them.

☐ Avoid comparing your objectives and progress to those of others. Moving at your own pace gives you the advantage of greatly increasing your chance of success when you establish the ground rules.

☐ Decide on a tempo.

☐ Follow up frequently.

☐ To stay confident, don't be scared to adjust your timeline.

Be An Observer

How well do you observe things? It's a crucial ability that's necessary for both learning new skills and identifying the parts of your current skill set that require improvement. How can you strengthen your capacity for observation? Contrary to appearances, this is not a skill that either you have or you don't.

The advantage of observational abilities? As was mentioned earlier, a key aspect of advancing your development is your capacity for self- and other-observation.

You will have a deeper understanding of who you are, which will make it easier for you to make decisions, chart your route, and develop the talents you need and want for success. You can choose your next objective thanks to the power of observation. Making an informed choice about your future, whether it be developmental or not, is essential.

❑ Looking at someone you respect, appreciate, or who inspires you is one of the best methods to sharpen and improve your observational skills. Examine their actions and consider their morals, ethics, and abilities.

☐ Even if it's crucial to avoid doing so, it can be beneficial to analyze what you value in others and how your abilities compare to theirs. It's not to make yourself feel bad; rather, it's to have a better understanding of what has to be done to bring you where you want to go.

☐ Another fantastic technique to hone your observational skills? Check out the crowds! What better way to exercise those talents than to have a nice beverage in a bustling cafe while observing others go about their day?

☐ Use your notebook as a space to reflect on and watch yourself in order to focus on yourself.

Seek An Interactive Environment

Engage in a range of social activities and community involvements to meet new people, learn about their backgrounds and personalities, and discover fresh perspectives. Additionally, there is an opportunity to network and form stronger connections; you never know how those things might advance your plans and objectives. You become a more adept navigator of the world and you start to recognize changes more quickly the more you interact with your environment.

- How would this help you? You become more receptive to new ideas and notions when you are more open to an interactive environment. That not only helps you become more open-minded, but it also enhances your capacity to learn new things and discover new facets of who you are.

- What settings do you frequently avoid but frequently enter? begin contributing.

- If you don't regularly have access to any interactive surroundings, you'll need to look for any on your own. You might start by looking online to see what potential events or activities are available nearby. Look for local online groups where you may post and inquire about these events or where people are discussing them.

- Pick one to begin with and go to it. Make sure to approach individuals and put yourself out there. Set a goal for yourself to speak to one person, three people, or five people if this is something you struggle with.

Measure Your Achievements

If there is one thing you have to do as you work on your personal growth, it is track your results. You can adjust your objectives and plans by doing this.

You must be adaptable and alter things up if they are no longer functioning. Measuring your successes and documenting your progress is the most effective approach to do this because it is the only way to ensure that you don't go down the incorrect path.

The advantage of doing this is obvious: tracking your accomplishments will help you stay on course. When you become aware that you have veered off the course you set for yourself, it tests your ability to come up with sensible answers. Lessons can always be learned, and by checking in, you can carry those lessons forward.

☐ You may choose when and how frequently you want to check in with yourself once you have a plan in place.

☐ Setting regular milestones will make it simpler to measure your accomplishments and will keep you motivated. Make it a practice to identify checkpoints for each objective you set for yourself.

Stay Honest

The best course of action is to be honest, especially when dealing with yourself. You can argue your point of view until you're blue in the face, but nothing will change. The hardest pill for most folks to swallow is probably that one. Reading a book or blog post about personal growth is far simpler than sitting down and being completely honest with yourself about your shortcomings.

Sure, the book might help you understand something or offer you a direction for moving forward. But if you don't sit down and be brutally honest with yourself, you'll never be able to put that knowledge to use to bring about genuine change.

When you pick up a book and tell people you're trying hard to be present, but when you're with friends and family, you instantly open social media on your phone, you're not really trying that hard, are you?

- No, you're just learning about it from a book. Being truthful with yourself about who you are and how you are doing is important.

- Include being honest in your routine check-ins and reflections. Just be honest with where you are in your journey and what you can do to guarantee you stay on the route you have set out for yourself. It isn't about beating yourself up or tearing yourself down.

Be Consistent

Consistency is the key to success in everything, including developing a balanced sleep schedule, food, and exercise program. You must be consistent in whatever you do if you want to develop good habits and attain your goals.

Consistency guarantees that you produce higher-quality outputs, are more effective, can monitor progress and success more easily, can spot improvement areas more quickly, and can be more successful overall.

- Focus on a single objective to improve your consistency. It can be difficult to establish consistency at first, which is why it's crucial to concentrate on just one thing. After it has stabilized, you can go on to the following objective or problem you want to solve.

- The importance of incremental progress stems from the fact that good habits don't just appear. A new habit might take months to develop, and that demands a lot of effort, perseverance, and focus. Celebrate each success you have to keep yourself inspired.

- You must develop coping mechanisms for your emotions because they can deplete your energy. Sometimes you're completely worn out, and other times your mind is playing games. Recognize that while your feelings are real and legitimate, they may not always be accurate. similar to how you might feel when you witness someone making out with your lover. Your feelings are legitimate, but just because you're envious doesn't mean your spouse is keen on returning the favor. Do not be fooled by it!

- If you mess up, you need to accept it and move on.

Self-Assess

Have you ever observed that there are occasions when it seems as though others understand you more fully than you do? Many people live in that reality, but it doesn't have to be that way, and more importantly, it shouldn't be that way.

No one should understand you better than you understand yourself, but if you want to understand yourself, you must give it some thought. Realizing how blind or how awful your behaviors have been can be an eye-opening experience, and even the greatest among us can experience this.

- Knowing your blind spots is important because everyone has them. By constantly growing and developing, self-assessment helps you become a more capable person. How do you rate yourself, exactly?

- Describe your observations.

- Examine what you observe.

- Asses what you observe.

Be Realistic

Although being positive is a good thing, you shouldn't be so positive that you come off as naive. Contrarily, that does not imply that you should dissect every imperfection or problem you possess.

There is a balance to be struck, and in order to do that, you must be realistic and well-aware of yourself. What are your areas of strength then? Knowing that is crucial, but so is being aware of your shortcomings and knowing how to strengthen them.

- Although being positive is a good thing, you shouldn't be so positive that you come off as naive. Contrarily, that does not imply that you should dissect every imperfection or problem you possess.

- There is a balance to be struck, and in order to do that, you must be realistic and well-aware of yourself. What are your areas of strength then? Knowing that is crucial, but so is being aware of your shortcomings and knowing how to strengthen them.

Make Good Judgments

Your life's course will be decided by the choices you make. One bad choice might not have much of an impact, but a string of them might. Making decisions with confidence is important, but you also need to make wise decisions.

Making wise judgments is the only way to continue on the desired course, despite the rewards being clear. It isn't as difficult as you may believe, nor does it have to be. Making wise decisions is actually a rather simple procedure once you know what to do.

☐ Pay close attention when you are hearing.

☐ To transform knowledge into comprehension, read critically.

☐ Observe nonverbal signs to understand what people aren't saying.

☐ Have individuals you can trust to give you advise; they will tell you what you need to hear, not what you want to hear.

☐ Recognize many points of view, explain them, and develop an acceptance of them.

Start Right Now

It's never too late to begin your personal development path, but there is no reason to put it off any longer now that you know what to do.

Career

Discover What Fulfills You

You will be more happier with your life if you can find a career that makes you happy. If you enjoy what you do, the hours will pass quickly. The fact is that it is a luxury and that not everyone enjoys it. What should you do if you're not happy in your job but are unable to make the necessary adjustments?

Finding your source of fulfillment would be the first step. You can determine how that pertains to your career once you have a firm grasp on it.

For instance, even though your profession doesn't scream service to others, you find fulfillment in helping others. You may say that someone working in the hospitality sector accomplishes that goal, but they might not be making enough money to support themselves.

What responsibilities at work enable you to satisfy that aspect of yourself? Can you consider how you relate to your coworkers and how you might assist them, or is there a part of your employment that includes serving others? If you want to find the fulfillment you've been looking for, you might be able to make that a bigger part of your role.

☐ If you're fortunate enough, you can steer your career in that way once you figure out what makes you happy, even if it means starting from scratch. Which is more important: being paid or finding fulfillment? We talked about your hierarchy of needs, and as long as you can take care of the essentials, you should be pursuing fulfillment. Starting again is occasionally the best thing you can do for your own development. It will be challenging, and it might take some time, but once you get where you want to go, everything you've ever wanted will be yours. You must devise a plan to do that.

☐ If all else fails, you can find hobbies that offer you that fulfillment while you work towards a career that can do the same.

Find A Mentor

Up and coming employees are frequently urged to locate a mentor within the organization in professional contexts. This mentor should be someone who is already established in their field and can provide direction and advise as needed.

What road are you on, and who else around you is taking it, as far as your professional personal development is concerned? Never undervalue the influence of sound counsel. Your career can advance in the direction of your desires if you make the proper decisions and brush up on the necessary skills with the aid of a mentor.

It's important to keep in mind that your mentor should be someone you get along with as well as someone you trust to push you if you aren't doing what you should be.

You shouldn't pick someone who is only one step ahead of you because doing so puts you at risk of coming off as competitive, which could cause problems. Select a person who is influential enough to be able to provide you with useful guidance.

What makes a mentor so great? They have already experienced everything, so they can give you a realistic assessment of the route you want to take. You can create a strategy to develop the necessary skills to pursue it if you have a clear understanding of what to anticipate. Additionally, getting to know others is beneficial, and establishing a mentorship relationship promotes you.

- If no one at work is available to help, consider looking for a mentor within the business. Although it isn't the best situation, it will undoubtedly help you on your road to personal development. Nobody can help you choose your career route as effectively as someone who has already taken it.

Make Yourself Likable

You should, on the one hand, not give a damn about what people think of you. You shouldn't base your choices on what other people think or what they expect of you. But it's possible to be likable and still be true to yourself. I'll tell you why.

The Wall Street Journal reports that studies have demonstrated that likability is one of the most important variables to boost your chances of promotion or employment (https://www.wsj.com/articles/why-likability-matters-more-at-work-1395788402). What more advantageous benefit can you imagine?

You can understand why it's important to blend in with the company culture from this. Your starting point is there.

☐ The next thing you should do is examine your personality and think about whether or not your actions might be offensive. Do you, for instance, feel the need to reprimand others when they speak improperly or choose the incorrect word?

Even though you may not even be aware of it, you do it at every meeting, and while you may have the best of intentions, your coworkers detest it. Even though it seems insignificant, it makes you look bad.

☐ You may improve your likeability while being true to who you are. That doesn't imply you have to change who you are completely or act unauthentically at work. Simply focus on developing the positive aspects of your personality and eliminating the unpleasant tendencies that could offend or irritate others. Another excellent example is someone's dedication to being truthful at all times.

Honesty and rudeness are not the same thing. Therefore, it is not being honest but unpleasant if someone goes out of their way to comment on someone's weight gain/loss or a change in style.

☐ Start focusing more on how you communicate with others and how those seemingly insignificant details may affect how they perceive you. Bad behaviors can be changed at any time.

Seek Feedback

You can use this point to support the previous one. If you frequently ask for input, it won't take you long to develop a clear image of what people think of you. That will help you address any negative behaviors you may have, but it will also enable you to seize any missed opportunities.

Offer anonymous responses when you do ask for comments so people can be honest. It's up to you to take the helpful criticism positively and brush off the trivial points. The more input we solicit, the simpler it will be to accept.

Looking for recurring statements will help you better understand what to do with feedback. Even if you don't believe it, you can't ignore it if half the responses mention the same thing. It's acceptable to argue that a crude remark made by one individual can be dismissed.

Don't ask the same people again, and don't pick those you think will respond favorably. Sincere reactions are what you need from feedback since without them, you won't be able to improve as a person.

This is about personal growth, and in order to grow, you need proper knowledge.

- [] The advantage of getting feedback is getting a different perspective on who you are as a person. Truth isn't always crucial; perception can sometimes be more significant. How are you seen by others? If you don't ask, you won't know, and once you do, you'll be unable to effectively control their perceptions.

- [] You can set up a box for people to leave their completed forms in and provide blank forms for everyone to take. No one will ever know who said what. As an alternative, you may create a Google Docs form that permits anonymous submissions.

- [] Create an action plan based on the feedback to further your project.

Skill Building

Building your skills is the main objective of personal growth. Therefore, it makes total sense for you to concentrate on developing your skills. The feedback you requested in the previous sentence ought to serve as a decent starting point.

You have probably recognized a number of chances or weak places as you work on your personal growth. You can determine which of those things to prioritize with the help of the comments you receive.

Your level of self-assurance will increase as you put more effort into developing your skills. Your confidence improves as you mature. Your sense of self-worth rises as you mature. Your new or improved skill set, together with all of that, will help you in every area of your life, but especially at work, where self-assurance and a solid skill set are crucial.

Therefore, the advantage of developing your skills is instantly noticeable in your self-assurance and respect. Beyond that, you will appreciate being able to perform your duties more effectively than you ever have. Focus on developing the skills that will help your career the most rather than honing those that you have already mastered or developed to an excellent degree.

What qualifications are necessary for you to advance in your career? You should concentrate on it since personal development is about pushing yourself, and you need those skills to advance to the next level. You'll need to strike a balance between stretching your abilities and considering the criticism you got.

There are several abilities you may develop now to help you advance to the next stage. The biggest benefits come from transferable talents since you can employ problem-solving, communication, and critical thinking wherever. Leadership skills are also portable.

☐ Select the three particular abilities you want to hone.

☐ Make a plan of action for how you intend to hone those skills.

Learn To Lead

Even though we only touched on it in passing in point five, this skill is significant enough to warrant its own heading. Your ability to manage, lead, and organize will serve you well wherever you go since leadership abilities will follow you there.

No matter how far up the ladder one climbs, a strong leader is always prepared, sets a good example, and understands that there is always opportunity for improvement.

Giving and accepting feedback, delegation, organizing, and inspiration are all examples of leadership abilities that were highlighted in point five. Problem-solving and communication were also addressed. An effective leader knows when to step back and when to take the initiative. They also know which chores to take on themselves and which to outsource.

To become a better leader, concentrate on developing those kinds of skills. Whether you currently hold a leadership position or not is irrelevant. In fact, it makes no difference if you aspire to a leadership role.

You don't need to hold a formal position of authority to lead if you have the necessary talents. No matter what position you have in life, you will benefit from all the qualities that make a good leader.

Your time management, productivity, and even the quality of your work will all increase as a result of developing your organizational abilities. A team's overall quality of work and productivity will increase by knowing when and to whom to delegate.

- You can motivate others and yourself if you have the skill to do so. Giving feedback in the right way enables you to support others on their path to personal growth, which will aid you on your own journey.

- Select the three particular abilities you want to hone.

- Make a plan of action for how you intend to hone those skills.

Learn Something New

Make every day an opportunity to learn something new by picking up a book on personal development or listening to a podcast about being a better version of yourself. You'll be able to perform better in your work and in your personal life if you develop this habit. Every day presents a new opportunity for learning, therefore, you should make an effort to do so.

Make it your goal instead of waiting for someone to send you a link or teach you something. We are often guilty of sitting around and waiting for chances to present themselves rather than pursuing them. When we're bored, we prefer to wait for someone to text us rather than talking to someone.

Instead of creating our own lives, we wait for them to happen. The same is true of knowledge. Your fingertips are on it!

☐ Create a schedule for the upcoming week (or month), and assign yourself a daily learning task. The day after that, you can research the artist you've always admired. Tomorrow, you can discover the word's etymology. What matters is that you make an effort to increase your knowledge; it doesn't matter what you learn explicitly.

The advantages of doing this are numerous; in addition to having all of this new knowledge, you will gain confidence, be more open to learning new things, and probably be able to hold a conversation better.

☐ Make some notes on what you've learnt and how it has helped you after the first week. You'll want to maintain this habit, and the easiest way to do so is to prepare in advance. Maybe you'll decide on a book and resolve to read a chapter of it every day until you finish it.

Improve Your Weaknesses

Start by viewing your weaknesses as an opportunity to improve rather than a threat. You shouldn't be surprised that I'm recommending it because that's what personal development is all about.

An essential component of the self-improvement journey is developing the self-awareness required to recognize your weaknesses. A further example of personal development in action is the fortitude it takes to modify and strengthen your areas of weakness.

The advantages should be clear as you are addressing your perceived shortcomings and making them less noticeable. In interviews, when the inevitable question about your greatest strengths and largest shortcomings arises, there is also a strength in character you demonstrate by addressing your weaknesses.

You cannot become better without improving your skill set. Make an effort to overcome your inadequacies by taking specific action. You'll advance personally, enhance your skill set, and serve as an example for others around you. But you don't have to go that far; you can just take baby steps to get better. Ideally, you can make them your greatest strength.

- Self-awareness training is the first step to overcoming your flaws. You can achieve this through journaling, giving names to your feelings, or even by practicing meditation.

- Ask a friend or family member for advice. Someone who can point out your weaknesses that you might not have otherwise seen. You can create a strategy to strengthen your shortcomings once you've identified them. It's not necessary to be an expert in every field. You might have developed a product, but your sales abilities are subpar. Even if you have staff to handle your company's sales, you still need to be able to communicate with investors, so you concentrate on honing your sales abilities.

Professional Development

You can concentrate on professional growth to work on self-improvement in the same way that you wish to build a variety of talents. It's crucial to continue performing at your best in work.

Many firms are cautious to spend money on conferences and seminars for staff members that aren't required. To stay competitive in your field and advance your skills, you can work on your own professional development. It's up to you how you accomplish it, but it can involve reading books on your field or listening to podcasts about it.

The advantage? Long-term achievement. Since the world is changing quickly, it is essential for you to stay on top of your game if you want to achieve long-term success.

Keep up with your sector if you want to be a fantastic candidate for a promotion or new employer. Education doesn't end with school.

- Look for books, podcasts, and webinars that can help you advance your knowledge and abilities in the workplace.

- Look for senior employees in your firm who now hold the position you hope to fill one day, and ask if you can shadow them to learn more about what their day entails.

☐ Build a compelling business case for why your employer should pay for any training or conferences you specifically want to attend. Describe the advantages your attendance will bring to the firm and how you intend to use that knowledge.
Always research in advance so you can present your boss with a strong argument. If you still can't convince them, but it's something you *want* to do you will need to decide if you want it bad enough to pay for it yourself.

Learn To Motivate

Strong leadership and motivational abilities are helpful in any work and in any business, whether or not you intend to be a leader. Morale and productivity problems may arise if you lack the ability to motivate.

Even if you don't consider yourself a leader, there are many possibilities to inspire others. You should take the bull by the horns and make a change if you think that low motivation at work is preventing people from being productive.

It's advantageous for your professional development, your self-assurance, and the team's morale and output levels. You can ensure your business operates as efficiently as possible by being proactive and inspiring.

- People ought to be able to inspire themselves, but occasionally they require assistance in doing so. So, make it a habit to let people know what you need, when you need it, and why. The larger picture motivates people.

- Find out what they need to feel and participate. You have to appeal to each person specifically since we are all inspired by various things.

- Once you've given someone a task, give it to them. They are responsible for it, and if they have any questions, they can contact you.

- Say "thank you," "congratulate," and "perform well," and let your superiors know.

Relationships

Your Own BFF

We all struggle with treating ourselves with the respect we deserve, if there is one thing in particular. When it comes to our friendships, we find it simple to provide those close to us with the compassion and understanding they require during trying times. However, we find it difficult to have the same level of compassion for ourselves. So, my first piece of advice for personal growth is to be your best buddy.

Friendships are vital, but if you don't know how to treat yourself with kindness, how can you be confident that you treat others with kindness?

The advantage of becoming friends with yourself is that you will gain a deeper understanding of who you are, which will enable you to make more informed decisions and be more likely to be kind to yourself.

Additionally, when you practice self-compassion, your empathy will develop, which will improve all of your other connections and friendships. Another advantage of being your own best friend is that when you start the process of getting to know yourself, you'll have a clearer notion of the areas of your life you want to focus on improving to find fulfillment. It benefits both parties.

☐ First and foremost, set aside some quiet time for reflection to begin getting to know yourself better.

☐ You help your friend out when they are struggling by doing things for them. How can you lighten your own load? You should take that into account as you make the transition to self-friendship.

☐ Self-care is another fantastic skill you may use to strengthen your friendship with yourself. True and respect are the cornerstones of any enduring relationship, and by taking care of yourself, you are demonstrating your own respect for yourself. Do not undervalue the influence that knowledge possesses.

Set Relationship Goals

It matters how you interact with those around you. It matters how you treat others around you. Our interactions have an impact on our general wellbeing and health. Humans are sociable beings who seek out other people to interact with and form friendships with. You should think about setting objectives for your relationships in the same way that you would for your work. Relationships are crucial, but you can't just hope for the best.

Your personal connections resemble a garden. You must take care of it, which include giving it regular watering, weeding as required, pruning as needed, and preparing it for change.

If you apply that concept to your relationships, you must stay in touch, get together frequently, give each other harsh love when necessary, and support one another when things are tough. You're not in a healthy relationship if you can't do that.

Setting relationship objectives may seem like it wouldn't be a part of personal development, but I can promise you that it is. The way you treat people reveals a lot about who you are at your heart.

☐   However, we frequently just give our closest friends and family the scraps after taking care of everyone else. Your priorities are at stake here as well as your relationships.

- Make a schedule if you're prone to time slipping away or you have trouble managing your time. Include times for you to text, call, or meet your pal in that schedule (s).

- Put your phone aside, switch off the television, and focus entirely on your friends or family members when you are with them. Relationships are based on respect, trust, and honesty, and nothing emphasizes the latter more than letting someone know you are only thinking about them.

Look For The Best In Others

There are many people that struggle with this, which is understandable. When someone wrongs you, it's simple to hold back and believe that everyone will act in the same way.

Living like that is not a good idea. You must be optimistic and give others the benefit of the doubt. If you quit criticizing everyone in life based on the actions of one individual, you'll be much happier.

How would granting others the benefit of the doubt assist you? First of all, you will worry about someone's intentions much less frequently. If you think that everyone is out to get you, you don't need to panic. It's laborious. It's draining. I am aware of this since we have all experienced it, whether on purpose or not. It's so simple to slip into the trap of placing blame for one person's behavior on everyone else.

You must have made blunders in the past. You've undoubtedly caused upset, broken a few hearts, or amicably ended friendships. Do you want people to forever hold those things against you?

Even worse, even though you haven't engaged in any of those behaviors, someone else has encountered distressing circumstances and is now wary of you in case you act similarly. It's not just, is it? Let's quit holding individuals to an unreasonable standard and instead develop as people.

The beauty of this is that you'll treat people nicer, which will increase their faith in you. You'll be happier and more at ease managing your friendships. You might easily reach burnout levels of exhaustion if you constantly think that people are out to get you.

☐ Think about some of the people you don't trust or who you tend to presume the worst about.

Come up with facts that challenges your beliefs and challenge the reasons you believe what you do.

 When you catch yourself assuming the worst about someone, instantly list at least one advantage.

Make A Habit To Phone Home

Strong social connections are crucial. When we run headlong into a challenge, our closest friends and family are the ones who help us get back up, dust ourselves off, and inspire us to keep moving forward. Even if the idea of making a phone call every day might be intimidating, you can continue to text instead if that suits you better. Some folks have a tendency to talk a lot and may keep you on the phone for much longer than you can stand. The goal of this personal development activity is to demonstrate to people that you care about them by checking in with them.

Relationships are mutually beneficial, so if you want somebody you can depend on, you must also be someone they can depend on. When life becomes hectic, it is simple to forget that.

Additionally, I would advise holding regular family gatherings. Although these two things might appear to be independent, they are similar enough to be combined. It's worth sitting down for regular check-ins if you have a family of your own (or live with a spouse, partner(s), or roommates).

This is your chance to talk about your own goals, group goals, and any other issues that may arise, such as who is responsible for what chores or what significant events are approaching. It's wonderful to have a conversation with someone about how their life is going.

☐ We've already talked about drawing down a timetable that includes socializing. Use that calendar to arrange a daily phone contact (or even text conversation) with a member of your closest relatives or friends. Every day should feature a different person!

☐ Set up a family gathering and discuss your proposal there. Once you have everyone's support, you may decide how frequently and on what night to have family meetings. Once everyone has consented, you may schedule it. Make an agenda for your meeting and follow it to keep everything on course.

Properly Prioritize

Even though this is listed under relationships, your priorities may be different. You must decide which category something falls under based on your own preferences.

However, I made the decision to categorize it under relationships since, for the most part, we place the highest emphasis on our families and friendships. The issue with that is that it hardly ever comes through in our words and deeds. We count on our family and friends, and we count on them to be there when the time comes to pick them up. Regrettably, that can mean we miss out on events like games, meals, barbecues, zoo days, beach days, and other activities.

What, then is your top priority? Your children should come before anything else if you have any. Children require time and care in addition to a roof over their heads, regardless of who provides the family's income.

They are always there when you arrive home, but that does not mean you should put no work into them. I would advise you to fast-forward to your death if you are unsure of your priorities.

If you missed overtime, you probably won't regret it because you missed your daughter's game-winning goal or your son's heartfelt performance in the school play. If you stay late at work and miss those priceless moments, you will be sorry.

- The first step is to sit down and determine your priorities. Once you are aware of your priorities, you can stop and consider whether or not your activities are in line with them.

- Every element of your life benefits from time management skills, which you may learn to successfully prioritize your responsibilities. There are only so many hours in a day, but if you use them wisely, you'll discover that there is enough time to do all of your tasks.

Strive for Productive Communication, But Don't Be Shy of Debate

Arguing is a necessary element of communication, believe it or not. Arguments in healthy relationships are inevitable; it's just how life works. However, disagreements must be respectful and constructive in order to be productive. It's not name-calling and screaming insults at one another when you become angry.

By having the uncomfortable dialogues that we often avoid, we can burn off those surplus feelings. In a perfect world, you would address these discussions right away. Having saying that, disagreements aren't always bad.

Arguing is a necessary element of communication, believe it or not. Arguments in healthy relationships are inevitable; it's just how life works. However, disagreements must be respectful and constructive in order to be productive. It's not name-calling and screaming insults at one another when you become angry.

By having the uncomfortable dialogues that we often avoid, we can burn off those surplus feelings. In a perfect world, you would address these discussions right away. Having saying that, disagreements aren't always bad.

What images do you have in mind when you consider a debate? You're doing it badly if you're shouting, angry, or enraged. People frequently engage in arguments, which are really disagreements over ideas.

We tend to become agitated when someone holds a different opinion from us, which is why conflicts frequently turn violent. We should all have better control of our emotions, so they shouldn't have to and shouldn't.

Avoid speaking in a hurtful way to others. Don't shout to overpower someone else's speech. Give everyone an equal opportunity to speak. Giving each other the time and space to communicate openly doesn't require your agreement.

For personal growth and development, it's crucial to consider opposing ideas. If you judge someone's worth based on the beliefs they have, it can be tough to empathize with them. It's beneficial to having your opinions challenged because it makes you think about why you hold those opinions.

☐ What is troubling you? Direct your questions to the source, then sit down and discuss the situation with them.

☐ You must have the argument if you find yourself in one. Many people withdraw, thinking that calming down is the best course of action. Yes, I would think you should retire and calm yourself if you find yourself tempted to throw insults. However, if you both maintain composure, you can have the disagreement that is obviously necessary. If you keep scurrying off, the conversation will never be completed.

Know When To Apologize

The difficulty with saying "sorry" is that rarely do those who should apologize actually do so. Elton John wasn't lying when he said that. Those who don't need to apologize frequently do so instinctively. Who are you, exactly? No matter which side of the aisle you are on, you must learn when and how to apologize.

First and foremost, you should apologize right away to everyone you have offended, wronged, or caused harm to. Avoid mentioning "if," as celebrities have done while apologizing. There are no ifs, accept responsibility for your actions, and offer an unqualified apology.

You must accept accountability for your actions if you want to keep the trust in your relationships. Understanding when and how to apologize has this advantage. I want to show you how to apologize correctly before I give you actions to take in light of this point.

- **Show regret.**

When you apologize to someone, make sure they know what you're sorry for in order to demonstrate your sincerity. Be direct and leave out any ifs or buts.

- **Recognize Pain**

  You must admit that you hurt or distressed this person. By doing this, you demonstrate that you are open to their viewpoint.

- **Attempt to Forgive**

  Do not presume that simply because you apologized, you have their forgiveness. After expressing your heartfelt regret, you must formally request their forgiveness. Know that you can ask, but that doesn't mean that they need to give it.

- **Redemption**

  If the other person accepts your apology, you can then inquire about how you might make it up to them. This underlines your honesty and commitment to putting things right. So, inquire as to how you may make amends. They could be quick to forgive, but that doesn't imply they'll give you their trust back right away.

What Not To Do

Along with the aforementioned methods, there are some things you must avoid doing at all costs. Avoiding it was already mentioned, but you also shouldn't try to take the blame or excuse your conduct. These additions together lessen the apology.

- ☐ You probably owe an apology to someone right now. As soon as you're prepared, I want you to sit down and write them an apology (whether you give them it in writing or vocally).

- ☐ Start observing who around you apologizes right away and who balks. What does that reveal about the person they are, in your opinion? What are the takeaways from this?

- ☐ The most important thing is to be aware of how frequently, what, and how you apologize, as well as how others react to your excuses. You might learn some realities about your personality and conduct from this enlightening practice.

Be Accountable

On the previous point, this one builds. Your choices are entirely your own. It's critical that you accept responsibility for your acts, words, and thoughts since they are your own. There is no victim in you. By putting the blame on others, your situation won't alter. No matter what your situation, you must take responsibility.

There will be occasions when someone wrongs you and you have good reason to be angry. You still can't hold onto your rage in those situations because you owe it to yourself. The only person who will suffer if you hold onto your rage is you because doing so will only fuel hatred.

Thus, the advantage of making yourself responsible for your deeds, words, and ideas is that you gain control over your life. Your life is being directed in the right direction by you, the one in the driver's seat. You relinquish that authority when you don't take responsibility. The route to personal growth and development starts with you and taking responsibility for your choices.

☐ These actions will assist you in going forward with accountability. Consider a grudge you have harbored against someone because you consider them responsible for an event that happened to you. I want you to reinterpret the circumstance and own up to your role in it. For instance, you can be upset because your friend got the job you wanted before you did.

Although it's not their fault, it is your fault for the way you responded. Even though losing a job to a friend can be painful, a good friend can still celebrate their friend's achievement. You've intensified your anger and resentment as a result of holding a grudge.

☐ If you find yourself blaming someone else for your predicament or circumstances, stop right away and consider your part in it. Concentrate on the one thing you can control: yourself.

Control Your Negative Thoughts

You need to learn how to control your bad thoughts, whether you are a negative thinker or occasionally a victim of negative thinking. Negative thinking is the main obstacle that will prevent you from achieving your personal development objectives.

What advantages are there to learning to control your negative thoughts? An increase in self-assurance and self-worth! You'll feel more confident in your skills and abilities once you manage such thoughts. If you don't think you're capable of it, how can you pursue being the best version of yourself?

That's why you need to deal with those negative thoughts. It isn't enough to tamp them down, you have to correct them to let go of the residual feelings.

- You must correct your mind process as soon as you see it veering toward negative. This is a process that will carry on forever. It will get simpler to stop having negative ideas altogether as you confront and correct them more frequently.
- Negative thoughts will still cross your mind, but they won't have the same effect on you as they had previously. In time, you'll be able to dismiss a bad notion as quickly as you can swipe a

notification off of your phone, while once it might have been something that could throw you off course.

In fact, using that visualization technique might assist you deal with your negative ideas.

- Bad thoughts regarding other people are another element that might spark off a negative mindset. If you frequently pass judgment on others or harbor unfavorable thoughts about them, you must confront this behavior if you want to overcome it.

If you take charge of your thoughts, you'll be much happier and less critical of others. The good news is that you'll become a nicer person to be around and a better friend as a result.

Meal Planning

You might wonder how this advances your personal development, but believe me when I say it does. The benefits of meal planning are numerous. It will not only make sure you eat better and resist the temptation of bad food, but it will also help you manage your time more efficiently. You can make a meal plan in a number of different ways. Either sit down and plan a menu, then go shopping to make sure all the items are on hand. Or you may plan a menu, go shopping, and do as much preparation as you can in advance. You must choose the option that will work best for you.

Meal planning is meant to reduce a lot of the anxiety we feel when it comes to eating. How frequently do you inquire about the supper menu in your home? If your household is anything like the majority of households, it probably happens every day. Probably more time is spent considering what to serve for supper than actually preparing it.

In order to save time, effectively manage your food budget, and maintain your health goals, plan ahead. While meal planning does require some time, the time you will save by doing so will far surpass the time it initially takes.

- ☐ Write down all of the meals you prepare most frequently and that your family enjoys to get started. You should begin with a month's worth of meals, but since you're just getting started, start with two weeks.

- ☐ In the repeatable meal plan for a month, there should be a new meal for each of the 14 days. Everything relies on your preferences and how frequently you enjoy eating particular foods. This is your chance to try out some brand-new, nutritious, quick dishes while still enjoying your old favorites.

- ☐ After writing your plan, you may go shopping for all the supplies and begin prepping the vegetables. To get started, write out all of the meals you make most often and those your family love. Ideally, a month-long meal plan is what you want to work with, but since you're new to the game start with two weeks.

There should be a different meal for each of the 14 days, in the month-long meal plan you can repeat. It all depends on your tastes and how often you enjoy eating certain things. This is your chance to experiment with new, healthy, easy meals as well as enjoying the favorites.

☐ Once your plan is written you can shop for all of the ingredients.

☐ Now you can prep vegetables in advance.

☐ Once mealtime rolls around you can simply throw it all together and cook it!

Exercise

Exercise is a fantastic tool for physical development, but it's also beneficial for your mental and emotional health. By exercising consistently, you are learning to develop healthy habits in addition to preserving your health, which is beneficial for both your confidence and health.

Any habit must be developed consistently, and if you can get into the routine of working out frequently, it will be simpler to develop other healthy routines.

How frequently should you work out? What kind of exercises ought you to perform? Well, that relies entirely on you. In the end, you shouldn't go more than three days without exercising. In a perfect world, you would schedule daily exercise and switch up your routine to prevent strain or injury. This does not require you to run 17 miles or lift weights for an hour.

Adults should engage in 150 minutes of moderate aerobic activity or 75 minutes of strenuous aerobic activity per week, according to the Mayo Clinic. Furthermore, you ought to perform strength training twice a week, making sure to target each muscle group (https://www.mayoclinic.org/healthy-lifestyle/fitness/expert-answers/exercise/faq-20057916).

- Do not force yourself to exercise all at once if it has been a while since you last did so. You can begin with a daily ten-minute workout and progress to lengthier exercises. If you start small and work your way up to the bigger things, you are far more likely to stick with it. Going too fast and hard will cause you to burn out and give up.

- Your daily routine is equally crucial. The best course of action is to pick activities you enjoy. If swimming is something you enjoy doing, consider doing that instead of running, which you detest. Choose a strength activity instead, such as hard gardening or hill walking, if you detest lifting weights.

Manage Your Sleep Pattern

How many hours do you sleep at night? The typical adult need between seven and nine hours of sleep per night. What is your secret code? You may be able to recall off the top of your head that the ideal amount of sleep for you is seven hours, 32 minutes.

Try some experiments if you're unsure of how much sleep you need for the best results. Every night, go to bed at the same hour. To discover your magic number, try waking up at various times.

Why is sleep good for you? Regularly getting quality sleep increases efficiency and aids in the fight against stress and lifestyle diseases. You already understand quite well how groggy you feel the morning after a bad night's sleep. Imagine how challenging it is to function when you extend that over the course of a week or longer. Additionally, it increases your propensity to grab for caffeine, which might disrupt your evening sleep.

A bad night's sleep also increases your propensity to eat fatty, sugary foods in an effort to increase your energy. So, a basis of good health and happiness is getting enough sleep.

☐ This recommendation is quite straightforward. Once you are aware of your magic sleep number, all that is left to do is decide when time you will go to bed and wake up. For instance, if you are aware that eight hours of sleep are essential, you can set your alarm for six in the morning and go to bed at ten.

☐ Establish a sleep schedule that you adhere to each night before bed so that your body is prepared to rest when it is time. It's possible that you turn off all electronics an hour before night and read a book instead. Maybe a warm bath and a cup of hot milk are what you'd prefer, or maybe a quick yoga session would be better. whichever suits you!

☐ Even when you're not working or on vacation, you should get up and go to bed at the same times every day. Since consistency is so important, changing your routine over the week can disrupt your entire cycle.

Vitamins & Hydration

It's all about maintaining your health and fitness, which includes drinking plenty of water and eating a diet with the appropriate proportions of vitamins and nutrients. You should obtain all of the vitamins and nutrients you require if you consume a healthy, balanced diet. However, very few of us consume enough nutritious food to be certain, which is where fortified foods and supplements can tilt the balance in your favor.

The advantages of taking the proper vitamins are essentially about preventing the signs and adverse effects of vitamin deficiency. The CDC estimates that 10% of Americans suffer from a vitamin deficiency of some kind, with iron and vitamin B6 deficiencies being the most prevalent (https://www.cdc.gov/nutritionreport/pdf/4page % 202nd% 20nutrition% 20report 508 032912.pdf). What symptoms indicate a vitamin deficiency? Confusion, irritability, sadness, and decreased immune system are all signs of a vitamin B6 deficiency. In the meantime, an iron shortage (which is more common in women) can result in weariness, itching, pale complexion, and shortness of breath.

How do getting adequate water and consuming vitamins help with personal growth? Taking charge of your health and welfare is a necessary component of evolving as a person, and doing this is integral to that process. Ill health may result from failure to comply.

The best sources of Vitamin B6 include chickpeas, fish, poultry, and fortified breakfast cereals.

☐ Examine your diet to see if you are consuming the proper amount of vitamins and nutrients.

☐ Since you are meal planning today, you can make the necessary adjustments to increase your vitamin consumption. If your diet cannot give you with enough vitamins for any reason, choose supplements.

☐ You might want to consult your doctor first because they might advise particular vitamins or supplements for you. This and the point below will be covered in more detail because they are closely related.

☐ Keep a water bottle close at hand to ensure that you stay hydrated. Grab a glass of water rather than soft drinks, coffee, or energy drinks.

According to the Mayo Clinic (https://www.mayoclinic.org/healthy-lifestyle/nutrition-and-healthy-eating/in-depth/water/art-20044256), men and women should strive for about 3.7 liters of water per day. You should drink considerably more if you exercise frequently or live in a warm climate.

Take Ownership of Your Health

Your food, exercise routine, and sleeping patterns are just a few examples of how you are responsible for your health. When was the last time you visited a physician? The dentist, what about him?

There are certain regular appointments that we must keep as we age. appointments for pap smears, mammograms, skin checks, dental examinations, and physical exams. You must take responsibility for that and begin treating your preventative health seriously.

I shouldn't have to emphasize the advantages of caring about your health. You have an opportunity to detect illnesses early by making and attending to your regular checkups. It is simpler to cope with these problems the earlier you identify them. You might feel more at ease knowing that your checkups are current.

Never be embarrassed to discuss problems or worries with your doctor; after all, they deal with these things on a daily basis as part of their work. This is a crucial aspect of growing up, and by taking charge of it, you're accepting responsibility, which is a significant step in your journey toward personal development.

☐ Find out the examinations and appointments a person your age should have on a regular basis to get started. Once you are aware of when certain events should occur, you may schedule the proper appointments.

☐ ○

☐ Make a calendar and enter each appointment you have scheduled. You can add a reminder to the calendar for those appointments that you can't schedule in advance to help you remember when to take care of them..

Keep your scheduled times! Additionally, it's crucial that you come prepared with inquiries or remarks to make throughout your appointments. Nobody understands your body better than you do, and when you're in front of a doctor, it's simple to forget everything.

Environment

Vision Boarding

A vision board is a great tool for personal development since it collects all of your goals and aspirations in one location. It is a terrific reminder of what you want out of life to have your ambitions and dreams displayed someplace in your home (or online), and it will keep you on track.

With a vision board, you can set lofty goals and work backward to determine the best path to achieving them. By anyone else's standard, for instance, you are a successful person, but not by your own. An Aston Martin is what you desire most of all.

You simply won't feel as though you've achieved success until you have that car. The need for material prosperity could be debated, but that is not the point. Work backwards from what you desire to discover precisely what steps you must take to obtain the Aston Martin of your dreams.

You can accomplish it with each of your objectives, dreams, or desires.

◻ You must first develop a vision before you can design a vision board. What then is your life's purpose? What are some of your vision's important tenets that you can see written on your vision board?

◻ Simply pinning aspirational images to a board is insufficient. You cannot set up the board and then relax while waiting for results from life. You now need to take action to make it happen, but before you do that, you must first develop a plan. Create an action plan using the ideas from your vision board. Your objective is clear, but what will it take to achieve it? Plan it. Do this for each and every one of your pinned images.

◻ You must prioritize your goals once you have a plan in place for each of them. Which of these dreams holds the most significance for you? Any connection between them? You can decide how to move forward with that information.

Planning

Planning and organization abilities are something that can have a good impact on every element of your life. Both at home and in the office, it can be used. Your calendar is turned to the month view, and you schedule your time as far in advance as you can. Do one week at a time to begin with.

You can extend your plans as your confidence grows. Naturally, it will depend on your line of work. Some people find it difficult to make long-term plans because anything might happen at any time. You'll be able to judge how far in advance is ideal for you. Children's appointments, social plans, and errands, among other things, can be added.

To make a month at a glance is the goal. Planning promotes stress reduction, which is good for your physical and mental health.

You can make your daily to-do list using that month view plan. Keep your daily list as short as you can by crossing off each task as you do it. You will feel more agitated as it becomes bigger and seem more overwhelming.

☐ Create your week or month view calendar first. You can still schedule personal appointments and errands if your work cannot be planned that far in advance.

☐ Utilize your plan to establish the hierarchy of priorities. What must be accomplished, what must be done, what would be wonderful to do, what is urgent, what is significant, or what may be delegated?

☐ Create your daily to-do list for the following day using those two in combination. The best course of action is to make a fresh to-do list every evening for the next day. By doing this, you'll be able to prevent taking on too much or having to start again if plans change.

Organization

Planning and organization go hand in hand; they are complementary abilities. Building effective organizing habits in one area of your life will have a positive ripple effect on other areas as well. The more proficient you become at it, the more probable it is that you'll apply those talents to every aspect of your life.

For instance, if you keep your home tidy and organized and develop the practice of taking care of issues as soon as they arise, you'll start to set an example for others at work.

People that are more organized have superior time management skills, are punctual, fulfill deadlines, and are generally calmer. The failure to arrange will only increase long-term stress.

☐ Think for a moment about your routines and actions. What unruly behaviors prevent you from being organized? You can put those negative habits at bay and clear your mind by organizing your environment, but if you want to be consistently organized, you'll also need to take steps to get rid of those poor habits. Dealing with a poor habit, such as being late, will improve your organizing abilities and vice versa.

☐ Start organizing in the area of your home that is the messiest and least organized. Don't even consider starting another project until you finish this one because you can only work on one project at a time.

☐ After dealing with the first region, you can move on to the next one and so forth. Continue doing this until your entire house is organized. This is something you may say at work or even in your automobile.

☐ Now resolve to keep up this degree of organization. Set aside time if necessary, and don't be hesitant to ask for help. It is everyone's responsibility to keep the home organized if you live with others. One job per day should be your goal when it comes to organization; you'd be astonished at how quickly they mount up.

The Big Purge

Although it's a stage in the organizing process, you must continue doing this every year. You ought to conduct a cleanse when you organize your house. There should be a purge at least once per year.

It's time to get rid of anything you haven't worn, seen, used, played with, or cooked with in a year. Go through your closets, cabinets, toy chests, and even your kitchen cabinets. Say good-bye and get rid of anything you don't need or enjoy.

It's not healthy for your mind or soul to constantly view items that we frequently cling onto for far longer than is necessary when you open a closet or cabinet. Consider every purge as a fresh start and a chance to start over. This is diet minimalism, not minimalism in general.

We are so burdened by our material stuff, but it makes things worse when we hang on to things we don't even need, utilize, or even see on a daily basis.

☐ This may become your new pre-holiday or spring tradition. Choose a specified period of year when you know you will have the time and energy to complete your purge because only you know your energy levels and schedule better than anybody else. Your initial cleansing, nevertheless, starts right now. Therefore, take a seat and decide how you'll attack each of your storage areas one at a time.

　☐ Ask yourself the following questions about each item: When was the last time I used this?

　☐ Will I probably use this again?

　☐ Would someone else utilize it? Then give it away or gift it. Otherwise, recycle it or throw it away.

　☐ Of course, these questions have exceptions. A china set that has been passed down through the centuries, or a dress that you save for extra-special occasions. When dealing with things like these, employ common sense.

The Most Important Task

The most crucial duty you complete each day should be the first one. This will guarantee that you reach your objectives and stop you from putting things off. You run the danger of leaving those major duties for tomorrow when you postpone them until after lunch or the end of the day.

You never know what kinds of issues will arise and throw your plans off course. If a task is crucial, complete it as quickly as you can. Unfortunately, we don't use common sense as often as we should.

There are a number of advantages to forming this habit. The first major advantage is related to stress management: by completing major chores ahead of schedule, you may effectively control your stress levels. Additionally, your efficiency and productivity greatly increase.

The remainder of your day will go easily if you finish that major task early. Additionally, it's a great approach to strengthen your prioritization skills.

Procrastination is one of the habits that is most crucial to your personal growth if you have it.

You'll start prioritizing naturally when you get into the habit of doing the most crucial work each day. You will know you've succeeded when you are no longer need to give it much thought.

☐ Regardless of whether you're doing this at home or at work, you must be able to prioritize your chores when creating your timetable and to-do list. Do you have any pressing chores to complete before the deadline? Begin with the most crucial duty, then move on to the next crucial one, and so forth.

☐ By just setting an example for others and encouraging them to give it a shot themselves, you may also persuade those close to you to act in the same way.

Money

You might not think of your finances as an aspect of personal development, but it is because a lack of financial planning can cause a great deal of stress. How can you develop and grow as a person if you're constantly stressed out about your finances?

Finances play a crucial role in personal development because they can affect many different areas of your life. Here are a few reasons why finances are important for personal development:

- Financial stability: When you have control over your finances, you can reduce stress and anxiety in your life, which can help you focus on personal development.

- Goal-setting: Financial planning requires you to set goals and create a plan to achieve them. This helps you develop a sense of purpose and direction in your life, which can lead to personal growth.

- Self-discipline: Managing your finances requires self-discipline and self-control, which are important traits to develop for personal development.

- Flexibility: Having a solid financial foundation can give you the flexibility to pursue opportunities that can help you grow and develop, such as taking classes or starting a business.

- Freedom: Financial independence can give you the freedom to make choices that align with your values and goals, which can lead to greater personal fulfillment.

Finances are an important part of personal development because they can provide stability, discipline, flexibility, and freedom, all of which can help you grow and thrive as an individual.

Know Your Finances

How much focus on your finances should you give? How frequently should you check your finances? Each and every day! The only way to be informed about your financial status is to be aware of it. Even though it's a small thing, it can have a big impact. How often do you idly spend money?

We've all been guilty of it at some point: you go to the coffee shop, grab the biggest flavor latte you can find, and throw in an almond croissant while you're at it, not really knowing what's in your bank account.

Start paying closer attention to your finances. The advantage? There are a variety of advantages, but two stand out. The first is that if you pay attention to where your money is going, your finances will benefit. The second is that you will have far less worry because you are aware of where your money is going.

☐ This step's goal is to identify your spending patterns by examining where your money is going. That includes all of your credit cards and bank accounts. Therefore, whether they are paper statements or an online account, verify your account statements every day before moving further. This will help you understand both what is leaving and what is entering.

☐ The following step is to classify your expenditures. If you use a banking app, it probably performs this automatically, but it's your responsibility to make sure the classification is accurate. Both variable and fixed costs will be incurred by you. Before moving on to your variables, start with the fixed expenses to see what you can do without.

☐ Now you can use an app that tracks your expenses or serves as a budgeting guide. Find the free ones there are quite a few out there. You can tweak your spending now to cut out any unnecessary expenses.

Your Spend

You'll be relieved to learn that there aren't many steps to following this straightforward rule. After completing the aforementioned tasks, all that remains is for you to keep track of your expenditures and, most importantly, to spend less than you make. It should go without saying that the advantages are to avoid debt and aid in the development of your financial future, which takes me to my next point.

Your Emergency Fund

At any given time, an emergency is just around the corner for everyone of us. A broken pipe could cause flooding in your home, and a car accident could force you to miss months of work. Everything is possible, and when it does, you need to be prepared.

You must begin saving for an emergency fund, which should equal at least three months' worth of income but no more than six months' worth. You need money for whatever situation you encounter in order to manage the stress and cover any expenses that insurance won't cover.

Money (or the lack of) is frequently the source of many of our problems, so having a safety net may be really helpful when things are tough.

☐ The first step is to decide how much should be in your fund because the quantity will depend on your own circumstances. Look at your outgoings and base your decision there.

☐ The best time frame is six months; anything beyond that should go into your savings account. Although it could take some time to develop, you must start somewhere.

It's time to start saving now that you know how much you want to put aside. Calculate how long it will take and plan a monthly contribution to your emergency fund so that you can mark progress along the way. Don't invest it or lock it away because you need to be able to access it when you need it. Additionally, it must to be kept in a different account than your checking and savings ones.

- ☐ If you're putting together an emergency fund alongside a friend or partner, having a clear plan for what counts as an emergency is very crucial. What matters? property repairs auto repairs medical expenses? lost a job? You will be more likely to resist the need to waste it if you have a clear plan in place.

- ☐ You must make sure to replenish your savings if you use it to pay for an emergency.

Your Credit Report

You must start making it a routine to examine your credit report once a year going forward. Checking your credit report is necessary to ensure that your information is accurate, that you are aware of your credit score, and, most importantly, that your identity hasn't been stolen.

It's a good idea to check your credit report to get a better understanding of your finances. You can get better prices and financial services by raising your credit score. If fraud is discovered, you can challenge it right away to avoid more serious problems in the future. You can discover erroneous or incomplete data. Additionally, enquiries from creditors and lenders will appear on your credit record. You will be aware that fraud is occurring even if you haven't asked for credit. If you notice a name you don't recognize, you can ask your lenders if they employed a third party to conduct the search because they occasionally do so.

- Applying for credit before making a significant purchase, such as a new car or house, allows you to see exactly what your lenders will see. Therefore, you can get ready.

- No matter what time of year it is right now, put it in your calendar: starting now, you must complete these activities every January.

- Here is what you should check twice!

  - Check that the details that identify you, such as your name, address, date of birth, and social security number, are accurate.

  - Verify all of your credit accounts, both old and new. You should carefully review this section to ensure that all of the information is correct. It's crucial that any unfavorable information that can be regarded outdated has been removed after the right period of time.

☐ Examine both soft and tough questions. Your credit score is unaffected by a soft inquiry. as when you look up your credit report. When you apply for a line of credit, a hard inquiry is made, which appears on your credit report. They can lower your credit score and be present on your report for two years. Additionally, there will be a bankruptcy area, so if you have filed in the past, you must make sure this information is correct. Likewise with accounts for collections. This part will show up if any accounts have been turned over to a collection agency, therefore you must make sure the information is correct since this can affect your future ability to obtain credit.

Your Debt

Let's talk about debt if you want to discuss things that prevent you from improving and evolving as a person. Debt is crushing. There is no greater trap to get into than the one where you constantly use your credit cards to make regular purchases because all of your extra cash was used to pay off your credit cards from the previous month.

You have no idea how often this happens. If you've ever wondered in secret how someone with a profession similar to yours manages to have the newest clothes, the trendiest cars, and all the technology... So-and-so may only be reliant on credit. However, it is irrelevant; what counts is how you are living.

There are several advantages to paying off your debt, but the largest one may be that you'll have more money and be able to retire sooner. Your risk will go down while your credit score increases. Debt carries a lot of risk, including the possibility of repossessions and debt collectors. Living on the verge of bankruptcy while in debt is quite stressful. Let's work together to reduce your debt.

- ☐ You cannot settle your obligations before you are aware of who you owe money to and how much. List every debt you have, including any and all loans, credit card balances, mortgage or rent, and any accounts that may be in collections.

- You need to write the monthly payment and interest rate next to each of your loans. Write down your minimum monthly payment and interest rate next to each credit card. The minimum monthly amount you owe is calculated by adding the minimum loan payment to the minimum card payment.

- You can check your credit report if you're unsure of how many open accounts you have.

- Your total payment is what you must make each month to remain on top of your debts, but if it is all you make, you will never be able to pay it off. You've spent a lot of time thinking about your finances and creating a budget, so you need to figure out how much you could pay each month.

- What's left over after paying for your groceries, utilities, entertainment, gas, and bills? You can use an average if it varies. If you have any extra cash, you should use it to settle your debt. Start with the debt with the highest interest rate and concentrate on one debt at a time.

- Ensure you pay your bills on time.

Your Income

The potential for income growth comes together with personal development. You must take action if you have a problem with your income, such that it prevents you from meeting your financial objectives and paying your bills. I'd delighted to make an income recommendation for you, whether it be a side job or generating passive income. I want to assist you in making the most of your income because that is sometimes more realistic.

☐   First, pay yourself! Even if your income rises, you'll always be able to spend your money. Your pocket will only become empty as a result of the increased money. Paying yourself first is the best method to make sure you are saving money.

☐   Create an auto-deposit so that as soon as you receive a paycheck, your savings are deducted. If you are still establishing your emergency savings, take this into consideration. To make sure your payments are made on time, you can do the same for your debt.

☐   Create a bigger cash cushion in your budget. How can you reduce your expenditure so that you have a larger cash reserve at the end of the month?

☐ How much of your income is spent on acquiring stuff as opposed to creating memories through experiences? More material possessions won't make you a better person, but experiences can help you change. Spending on experiences rather than material possessions makes people happier.

☐ Remember to account for retirement! No matter how young you are, you must make arrangements for old age. Compound interest will be more advantageous to you the earlier your preparation starts.

☐ Hire a financial advisor to manage your finances and assist you in making the most of your money if you can afford to.

Recreation

Fun Matters

You've worked hard to grow yourself, and you're already halfway through this list. Although you should be happy with how far you have already gone, do you know what else is crucial? Fun!

If you tend to overachieve, this is even more critical. We only have one chance at life, so live it up. You deserve to. (If you tend to underachieve, you should probably cut back on the fun or at the very least improve your organizational skills so you can justify the time you spend having fun.)

Making time for enjoyment has a major stress-relieving effect. But it's also a wonderful chance for you to spend time with your loved ones. You can strengthen relationships with friends, family, and other people by doing this.

- ◦ We've already stressed how important it is to use your time wisely, so pay close attention now! Although you can arrange time for enjoyment, you don't always have to plan what you'll do during that time. I simply ask that you make sure to schedule time for enjoyment by including it in your plans.

◦ Make a list of all of your favorite interests, hobbies, and activities. You can consult your list for inspiration when it comes to having fun! Perhaps it's a season pass for the neighborhood soccer club, a poker night with your friends, or simply barbecuing with your friends. The only preparation you should make is to schedule a meeting time and location with other partygoers.

Going to the park to play catch is free, so you don't need to spend money to have fun. There are no ideal circumstances; enjoyment can be had whenever and wherever. Make fun of a behavior that is as automatic to you as brushing your teeth after meals.

Live, Laugh, Love - *Bonus!*

Just so you don't start rolling your eyes, I simply want to discuss laughter. The best medicine, they say, but how frequently do you laugh? I have a tendency to laugh a lot and loudly at just about everything because I genuinely like laughing. It improves my mood. You ought to want that for yourself, right?

Why not just join in and enjoy the tiny jokes along the way instead of being a serious person who rolls their eyes at the most watched sitcom on television?

You can instantly feel happier after laughing, and the more you laugh, the happier you will be. It is also beneficial to your health! Your muscles, heart, and lungs are stimulated, and your intake of oxygen-rich air is increased.

Of course, it also decreases the body's stress reaction and promotes endorphin release. You are aware of the advantages, but how can you laugh more?

- Set out with the intention of laughing, and make it a habit. Consider using a joke-of-the-day calendar or a meme-a-day to keep illness at bay. Follow accounts known for their ability to make you chuckle if you have a tendency of checking social media before you leave for the day.

☐ Why not watch stand-up comedians perform in addition to sitcoms? The selection of streaming services is almost usually wide.

☐ Do you know another amazing approach to making people laugh a lot? A pet! Pets make wonderful companions and are proven to be good stress relievers, according to a study.

☐ Plan a regular game night so you can spend time with the people you care about while having fun. Your friends and family are also a great source of laughs.

Final Thoughts

There are many things that link to personal progress; some of them you probably already know well, while others you might not have thought of as having anything to do with development. The appeal of personal development is that so many of these concepts and objectives are interconnected so that even if you focus on just one of them, the effects will spread to other facets of your life. Everything is related.

The ability to become the best version of yourself both personally and professionally is why self-improvement is so crucial. Several factors make self-improvement essential:

- Personal growth: Self-improvement can help you develop as an individual, enabling you to become more confident, self-aware, and fulfilled in your personal life.

- Professional development: Self-improvement can also help you progress in your career, develop new skills, and take on new challenges.

- Increased happiness and well-being: By focusing on self-improvement, you can increase your sense of purpose, satisfaction, and happiness.

- Better relationships: Self-improvement can help you develop stronger relationships, both with yourself and with others.

- Overcoming challenges: By working on self-improvement, you can develop resilience and learn to overcome challenges more effectively.

Overall, self-improvement is important because it can help you live a more fulfilling, successful, and satisfying life. By constantly striving to improve yourself, you can achieve your goals and make the most of your potential.

It suffices if you know yourself and keep moving forward rather than trying to balance every talent or quality you possess. You only need to evaluate, make changes, and continue.

Prioritizing and consistency should be the main goals in the start of your journey, and if you struggle or fail, you should just get back up and try again. Stagnation is the number one enemy of personal growth, so keep moving.

www.ingramcontent.com/pod-product-compliance
Lightning Source LLC
Chambersburg PA
CBHW070747220526
45467CB00018B/1022